Inventive Metal clay for beaders

Inventive Metal clay for beaders

Exciting projects for all levels

Irina Miech

Published by Kalmbach Publishing Co., 21027 Crossroads Circle, Waukesha, WI 53186.

X-ray photography by Albert Koetsier. Used with permission.

12 11 10 09 08   1 2 3 4 5

Printed in the United States of America

Distributed to the trade by Watson-Guptill

Visit our Web site at
www.BeadAndCraftBooks.com
Secure online ordering available

Publisher's Cataloging-In-Publication Data
Miech, Irina.
   Inventive metal clay for beaders :
   exciting projects for all levels / Irina Miech.
      p. : col. ill. ; cm.
   ISBN: 978-0-87116-258-8
1. Precious metal clay–Handbooks, manuals, etc.
2. Jewelry making–Handbooks, manuals, etc.
3. Beads–Design and construction–Handbooks, manuals, etc. 4. Silver jewelry–Handbooks, manuals, etc. I. Title.
TT212 .M5434 2008
739.27

Contents

Intermediate Projects

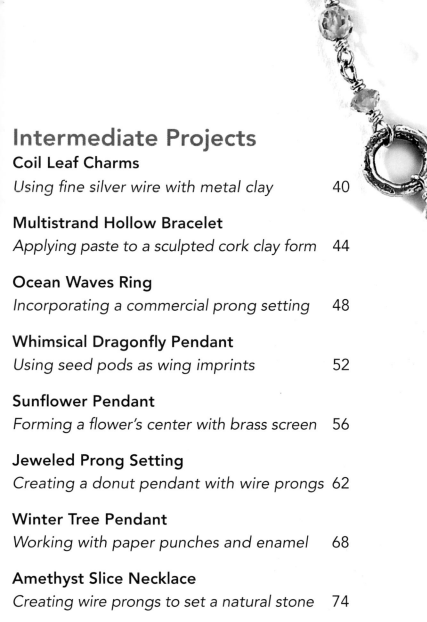

Advanced Projects

Inspiration and Creativity

EACH OF US DRAWS from a unique creative well. Most of my artistic inspiration comes from nature – from being outdoors and taking in all the natural beauty that surrounds us. When I go for walks with my family, I always come back with some little gifts of nature. I pick up leaves, pods, sticks, pieces of bark, shells – all kinds of interesting textures and forms that cross my path.

What kinds of things inspire you – certain surroundings, a season, styles of music, a part of the country?

Vacations near the ocean particularly enrich my creative well. The beach and the water can be tremendous sources of creativity. Everything about the sea inspires me, from the waves to the sand to the tidepools.

I love looking for rocks and shells on the beach and watching sea life. When I snorkel, it's as if a window has opened into a mysterious second world; I can look down and see an entirely different realm of texture and color. Sea urchins, fish, rays – they are all beautiful, and their forms fascinate me.

The photographic work of Albert Koetsier excites and inspires me. He explores the interplay of science and nature in his beautiful and sometimes mysterious X-ray images of plants, shells, and other organic subjects. His work is featured throughout this book.

Most of my artistic inspiration comes from nature.

Left and opposite: Tony Miech photos

Vacations near *the ocean* particularly enrich my creative well.

A sketchbook can be very helpful for recording impressions and ideas, and helping you translate your inspiration when you get back to your home or studio. I don't always sketch on the spot. When I see something that interests me – a shell, a tiny sea star, a flower – I try to hold it in my mind until I have the time to sketch it. I continue working with these thoughts, developing designs before I commit them to paper. When I find quiet moments in the day, I record ideas in my sketchbook.

It's very peaceful, almost meditative, to let the ideas evolve as I draw. I try to make detailed sketches of the exact pieces I want to create, but when I don't have enough time,

I draw a very rough sketch and write down a few words that will remind me of my original idea.

Inspiration dwells everywhere. I find it in teaching as well. Teaching always involves an exchange of ideas, which produces a synergy between teacher and student that I find very energizing. As I introduce students to new techniques, a new world opens to them. I become part of their excitement and joy, and I always learn something new. Keep yourself open to new opportunities, new activities, perhaps just a new route to take during your day.

Even mistakes can be opportunities for learning experiences. At times when I can't quite match the concept I set out to create, I often discover a very different idea in the process. Has this ever happened to you? It's good to stay open to these creative "mistakes." No time spent in creative pursuits, doing what you love, should ever be called a failure.

I designed the projects in this book to give you the skills to help you fulfill your personal artistic vision. The book is arranged in order of difficulty, starting with Beginner

projects and moving on to Intermediate and Advanced projects. Learn my techniques by making the projects as presented, then use them as a springboard. My wish is that you take each idea in new directions to create your own version – or many versions! – of the concept.

To see what I mean, look at the photos that follow the step-by-step project instructions. You can create all of the variations you see there simply by building on what you've learned, combining techniques from different projects, and adding your own imagination.

I hope this book helps you dig deeper into the creative well inside you. May it open the door to many more inventive ways to create beautiful jewelry with metal clay than you have ever imagined!

Anna Miech

It's very peaceful, almost meditative, to let the ideas *evolve as I draw.*

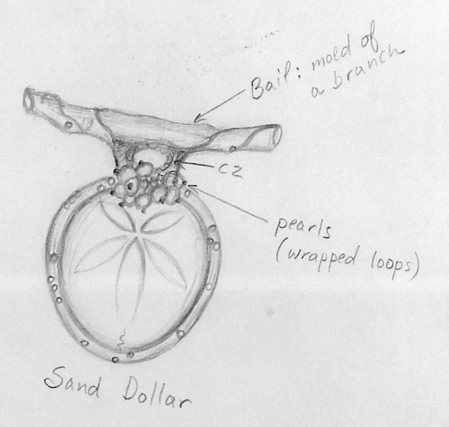

Bail: mold of a branch

cz

pearls
(wrapped loops)

Sand Dollar

beginner

projects

Spiral Pendant & Earrings

Spirals are one of the oldest symbols used in art, a visual depiction of a journey deep into the self. I hope this project is the beginning of a wonderful journey as you discover the potential of metal clay.

Materials
- 10g PMC3 clay
- PMC3 syringe
- PMC3 paste
- 1 4mm cubic zirconia (CZ)
- 2 3mm CZs
- 80–90 3mm Swarovski crystal bicones
- 80–90 2mm fine silver or sterling silver beads
- Flexible beading wire
- 24-gauge sterling silver wire
- 2 in. (51mm) sterling silver large-link chain
- 24-gauge sterling silver head pins
- Sterling silver crimp beads
- Sterling silver hook
- Sterling silver ear wires

Supplies
- Cocktail straw
- Liver of sulfur (optional)

Tools & equipment
- Metal clay basics: balm, fine-tip paintbrush, flexible sanding pad, plastic mat, polishing pad, rolling rectangle, ruler, tweezers
- Kiln setup
- Polishing setup
- Jewelry tools: chainnose pliers, crimping pliers, roundnose pliers, side cutters

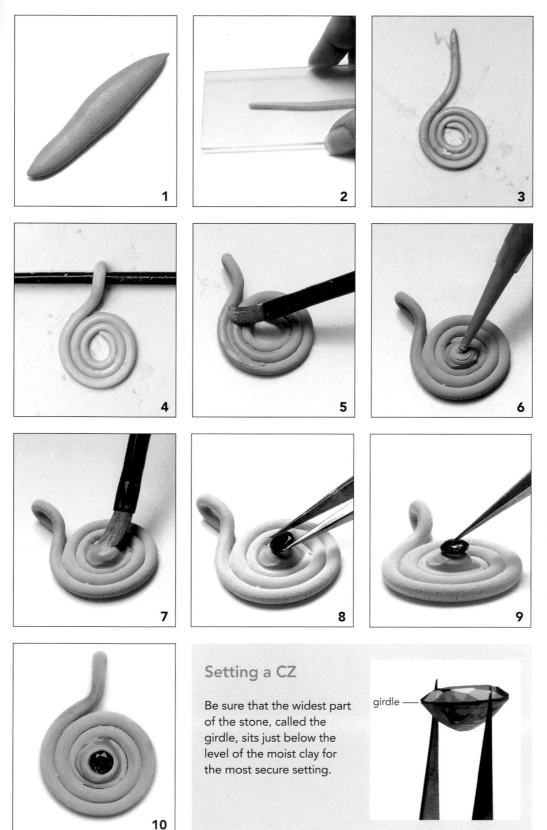

1 Shape about 3–4g of clay into a cylinder with your fingers.

2–3 Roll the clay with the rolling rectangle to about 6 in. (15mm) long with tapered ends. Apply extra balm to the clay and make a spiral, leaving about 1 in. (26mm) at the end.

4 To make the bail, grease a cocktail straw and form the end of the spiral around it. Adhere the tip in the back to create a closed loop. Dry completely.

5 Paint the entire piece with paste to smooth the shape, paying special attention to the joins, and let dry.

6–7 To set the CZ, wet the clay in the center of the spiral with the paintbrush. Using syringe clay, make a blob about the size of the CZ (or larger). Smooth with the paintbrush.

8–10 Using the tweezers, set the CZ on top of the blob and carefully push it in, making sure the girdle is below the surface of the clay. Let dry.

Setting a CZ

Be sure that the widest part of the stone, called the girdle, sits just below the level of the moist clay for the most secure setting.

girdle ——

11 For a finished look on the back, turn the piece over and wet the center. Using syringe clay, make a blob large enough to fill the gap in the center. Let dry completely, then sand with the flexible sanding pad. Fire, polish, and add patina if desired.

Decide how long you'd like your necklace to be, then add about 6 in. (15mm) to allow for adjustments and finishing. Cut the flexible beading wire to that length. For wrapped loop basics, see p. 108.

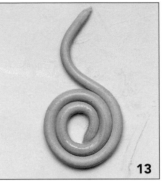

To finish the necklace

Necklace shown is 16 in. (41cm)
Cut a length of flexible beading wire and center the spiral pendant on the wire. String small silver beads and crystals alternately on both ends until you reach the desired length. Crimp the hook to one end and the chain to the other, reserving two chain links for the earrings. String a crystal on a head pin and link it to the end of the chain with a wrapped loop.

Earring components

12 Repeat steps 1–4, using about 2–3g of clay and rolling to about 4 in. (10cm) long.

13–14 Spiral the rolled clay, then shape the top loop with the paintbrush as shown, pressing firmly so the tip of the rolled clay adheres to the spiral.

15 Repeat to make a second spiral earring component in the mirror image of the first.

Dry completely, then follow steps 5–11 to finish two earring components.

To finish the earrings

Open the loop on one of the ear wires and attach a large link from the chain. String a crystal on silver wire and link it to the spiral component and the chain link with wrapped loops. Repeat for the second earring.

variations

Vary the bail design of your spiral pendant – you can even add a place to hang a bead tassel full of movement. By spiraling the clay around a larger cabochon, you'll create a bold focal piece.

Textured Frames

Using clay cutters and textured clay

This project is about creating complementary shapes and textures that not only work with one another, but also enhance the natural beauty of the pearls.

Materials
- 20–25g PMC3 clay
- PMC3 paste
- PMC3 syringe (optional)
- 2 10mm coin pearls
- 12 assorted pearls, 4–8mm
- Flexible beading wire
- Sterling silver crimp beads
- 2mm fine silver or sterling silver beads

Supplies
- Round toothpicks
- Liver of sulfur (optional)

Tools & equipment
- Metal clay basics: balm, files, fine-tip paintbrush, flexible sanding pad, plastic mat, playing cards, polishing pad, roller, scalpel
- 1-in. (26mm) flower-shaped clay cutters (various styles)
- ½-in. (13mm) circle-shaped clay cutter
- Rubber stamp mat
- Kiln setup
- Polishing setup
- Jewelry tools: crimping pliers, side cutters

Use a different shape of cutter for each flower.

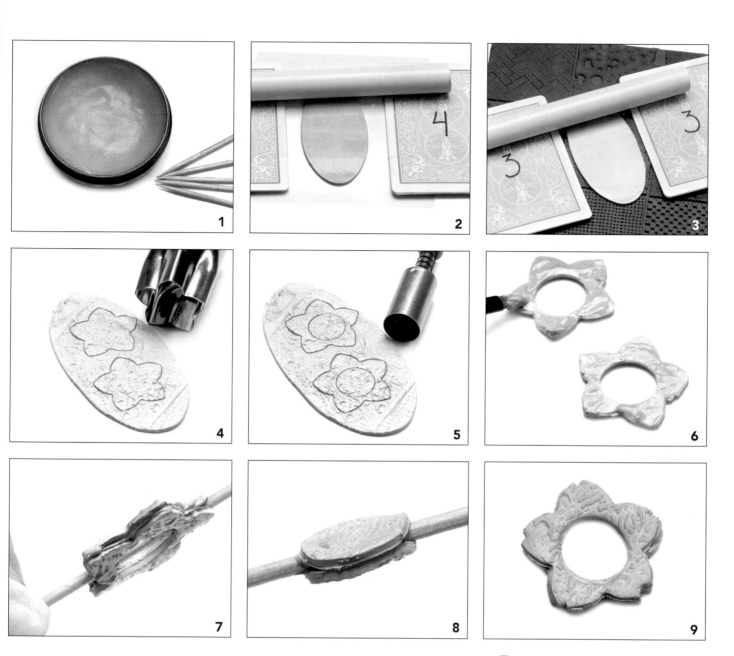

1 Grease five toothpicks generously.

2–3 Roll the clay to the thickness of 4 cards and large enough for two flower shapes. Add texture by rolling the clay on a rubber stamp mat to the thickness of 3 cards.

4–5 Punch out two flower shapes. Use a round cutter to punch out the centers.

6–7 Attach the two shapes together with a generous amount of paste, placing a toothpick between them. The paste should ooze out along the seam; otherwise you may need to fill in the seam with syringe clay.

8 Repeat steps 6–7 with the "hole" components (the round pieces you punched out).

Repeat steps 2–8 to make a second set of components. Use a different shape of flower cutter if desired.

9 To make the clasp, repeat steps 2–5. Attach the two flower shapes together with paste, this time without a toothpick between. Use the centers to create a third round component as before.

This is a good project for experimenting with different textures. Try stamps, texture plates, lace, leaves, and other surfaces that interest you.

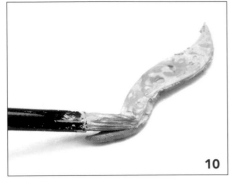

10

11

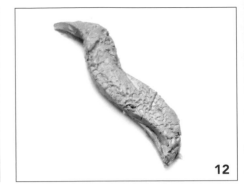

12

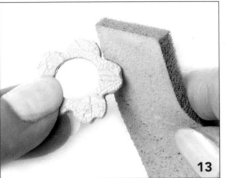

13

14

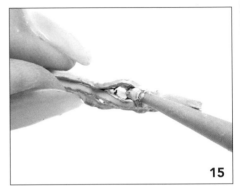

15

16

17

To finish the bracelet

1 Cut a length of flexible beading wire. Crimp the ring end of the clasp to one end of the wire.

2 String the flower and round components as shown, interspersing pearls and small silver beads. String coin pearls inside the flower components.

3 Crimp the toggle bar to the other end of the wire, adding a 5mm pearl on top of the bar. Trim the wire.

10–12 For the bar, cut a curved piece of clay out of the remaining textured clay, at least twice as long as the width of the toggle opening. Using a generous amount of paste, attach it to the remaining clay, smooth sides together. Trace the shape with a scalpel, cutting all the way through to make the toggle bar.

Let all the components dry completely, then carefully slide the dried pieces off the toothpicks.

13 File and sand all edges. Remember to smooth both the inside and the outside edges of the flower components.

14–15 If needed, moisten and fill any gaps with syringe clay or paste, leaving a hole for stringing. Let dry.

16–17 To create holes in the toggle components, insert the tip of the scalpel at a right angle and rotate it without applying pressure. Turn the piece over and repeat so the hole is even on both sides.

Fire, polish, and add patina to the pieces if desired.

Use only the hole components as beads, or focus on the flowers.

I often make a charm, sign the back, and attach it to the chain extender for a nice finish to a necklace. What will your signature charm be?

variations

Bisque-Core Beads

Using bisque cores to create metal clay beads allows you to keep the shapes and sizes consistent. Although the core doesn't burn away, it's lightweight and a good alternative to making hollow beads with cork clay.

Materials
- PMC3 paste
- PMC3 syringe
- PMC+ sheet
- Bisque bead forms
- Assorted kiln-ready CZs (optional)
- Casting grain (optional)

Supplies
- Chenille pipe cleaners
- Clear tape
- Elmer's glue (optional)
- Liver of sulfur (optional)

Tools & equipment
- Metal clay basics: fine-tip and extra-fine-tip paintbrushes, flexible sanding pads, needle stylus, polishing pads, scissors, tape, tweezers
- Paper punch
- Kiln setup
- Polishing setup

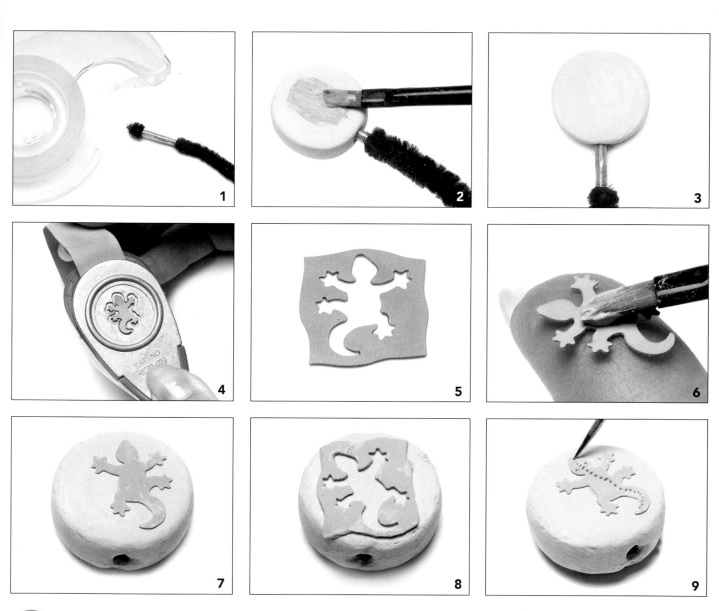

To make the shape stand out more against the bead, you can make it thicker by laminating the sheet clay: Fold a piece in half and adhere with Elmer's glue. Let dry and punch out the shape.

1–3 Wrap one end of a pipe cleaner with tape as shown. Insert into the bisque bead form and paint the bead with paste, applying five to ten coats. Dry the bead thoroughly between coats. It's a good idea to paint two to three coats inside the edge of the hole using an extra-fine-tip paintbrush.

4–5 Use a paper punch to punch out a shape from the sheet. Use scissors to cut around the negative image left by the punch.

6–9 Use paste to attach the positive shape to one side of the bead and the negative image to the other. Texture the shapes with a needle stylus.

When painting with paste, it's helpful to have more than one size of brush, including one with a very fine tip.

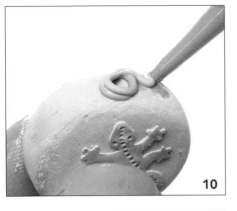

10

11

12

13

14

15

16

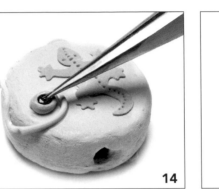

10 Using syringe clay, create coils to reinforce the opening of the bead on both sides.

11–16 You have several options for embellishing these beads. You can embellish with syringe clay or set CZs or casting grain. My example uses all three embellishments on one bead.

To embellish with syringe clay: Use your imagination! Always remember to moisten the area first.

To set a small (2mm) CZ: Moisten the area. Squeeze out a blob of syringe clay about the same size as the CZ and push the CZ gently into the blob using tweezers. Make sure the edges of the CZ sink slightly below the surface of the syringe clay.

To set silver casting grain: Use the same technique you used to set CZs.

Let dry completely. Fire for ten minutes at 1600°F (870°C). Let the kiln cool to room temperature before you open the door; do not crash cool the piece. Polish and add patina if desired.

variations

Don't limit yourself to making beads! Bisque cores are available in a wide range of shapes.

Try making a donut pendant that you embellish with the paper punch technique, or build the basic core shapes into interesting little sculptures. I made the acorn cap from dots of syringe clay.

Heirloom Spoon Bracelet

This project was inspired by rings made of actual spoons. Using molding compound and metal clay, you can create a collection of matching pieces from just one favorite spoon.

Materials
- 16–20g PMC3 clay
- 22-gauge half-hard sterling silver wire
- 12mm shell pearl
- 2 4mm and 2 7mm pearls
- Sterling silver toggle clasp

Supplies
- Two-part molding compound
- Spoon
- Clear tape
- Vermiculite
- Liver of sulfur (optional)

Tools & equipment
- Metal clay basics: balm, fine-tip paintbrush, flexible sanding pads, plastic mat, playing cards, polishing pad, roller, round metal file, ruler, sanding swabs, scalpel, scissors
- Oval bracelet mandrel
- Kiln setup
- Polishing setup
- Jewelry tools: chainnose pliers, roundnose pliers, side cutters

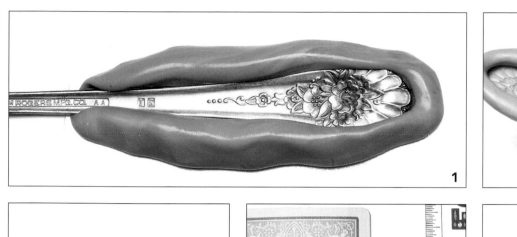

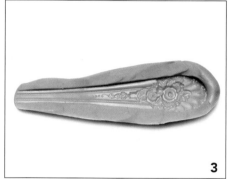

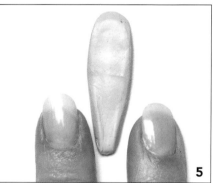

1 Combine equal parts of the molding compound, kneading them together until the color is uniform. Shape the compound to accommodate the spoon handle and carefully push the handle into the mold. Leave it in the material until the mold sets.

2–3 Lift the spoon handle out of the mold. If needed, trim the mold with scissors where it has folded over and covered the image.

To prepare the bracelet mandrel, tape a plastic mat to the narrow end of the mandrel and grease it.

4–5 Roll about 8g of clay to the thickness of 6 cards and about 2½ in. (64mm) long. Shape it to roughly match the shape of the spoon handle.

Explore antique stores or raid your grandmother's silverware drawer to find treasures to use as molds for this project.

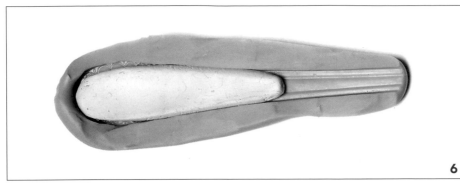

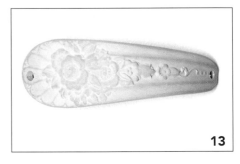

6–7 Using your fingers, carefully press the clay into the mold to fill it, touching both sides of the mold.

8 Lift the clay out of the mold and shape it over the narrow end of the bracelet mandrel. Repeat steps 4–8 to make a second component. Dry both completely.

9–11 Using sanding pads, smooth the sides and back of the components. If one component is slightly longer than the other, sand it until they're the same length. Use a sanding swab to smooth the details on the front.

12–13 Make a hole 2–3mm from the edge of each end of the two components. Insert the tip of the scalpel at a right angle to the piece and rotate it without applying pressure. Turn the piece over and

repeat to make the hole even on both sides.

Fire the components in vermiculite to preserve their shape. Polish and add patina if desired.

To finish the bracelet

Link the toggle loop to the first metal clay component with wrapped loops and pearls. Attach the second component to the first using a wrapped loop and the focal pearl. Finish by using wrapped loops and pearls to link the bar of the toggle to the second component.

Placing the small pearls near the clasp when you assemble the bracelet will taper the ends gracefully and make the toggle easier to open and close.

Using just the tip of the spoon for a mold yields a variety of patterned components. Don't forget about making a version of the spoon ring that inspired this project. How about a sweet, detailed bail?

variations

Leaf-Imprinted Beads

Leaves are one of my favorite motifs – they are timeless and versatile as a jewelry design element. Their organic texture adds natural beauty to your designs.

Materials

- 3–5g PMC3 clay per bead
- PMC3 syringe
- Casting grain
- Flexible beading wire
- Sterling silver toggle clasp
- 8 3mm Swarovski round crystals
- Crimp beads
- Sterling silver ear wires
- Sterling silver decorative head pins

Supplies

- Cork clay
- Round toothpicks
- Liver of sulfur (optional)
- Long leaves with well-defined veins, at least 1½ in. (38mm) long and ½ in. (13mm) wide

Tools & equipment

- Metal clay basics: balm, fine-tip paintbrush, flexible sanding pad, plastic mat, playing cards, roller, ruler, scalpel
- Kiln setup
- Polishing setup
- Jewelry tools: chainnose pliers, crimping pliers, roundnose pliers, side cutters

Spirea

1

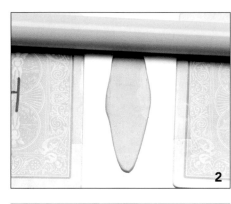

2

3

4

5

6

7

8

9

Sumac

1 Shape cork clay around a toothpick to about ¾ x ¼ in. (19 x 7mm). Let the cork clay dry thoroughly.

2–5 Roll the metal clay to the thickness of 4 cards. Place the leaf on top of the clay and imprint it by rolling over it at the same thickness. Remove the leaf and cut out the clay imprint with a scalpel.

6–8 Encircle the cork clay core with a trail of syringe clay and wrap the leaf-shaped clay around the core. It

helps to start in the midpoint and wrap toward the sides of the cork clay shape, working at a slight angle. As you wrap, shape the ends of the bead by pressing the clay gently into place with your fingertips. Use a light touch and a little water to avoid fingerprints. Let dry completely.

9 If any fingerprints show on the ends of the bead, gently sand them or plan to conceal them with embellishment.

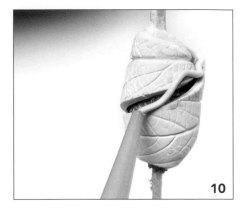

10

11

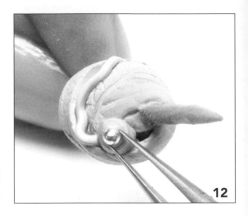

12

10–12 Embellish the bead with syringe clay and casting grain, taking care to close any gaps and conceal any imperfections. Use large pieces of casting grain to fill large gaps.

Dry the bead, fire, polish, and add patina if desired.

To create the bracelet shown, make three large, two medium, and two small beads. For earrings, make two small beads.

💡 *You can recycle your fine silver and metal clay scrap into casting grain by heating it with a torch. For more about casting grain, see p. 105.*

To make a bracelet

Cut a piece of flexible beading wire. Crimp the toggle ring to one end of the flexible beading wire. Alternate stringing crystals and leaf beads until you reach the desired length, ending with a crystal. Crimp the toggle bar to the other end.

To make earrings

String a crystal and a leaf bead on a head pin. Link it to an ear wire with a wrapped loop. Repeat for the other earring.

variations

Build a necklace from linked leaf-imprinted beads or create a dramatic silver focal bead. By allowing some space between leaves, you can build a stunning openwork focal as well.

Gilded Sea Urchin Set

This project was inspired by the amazing variety of sea life
I've encountered while snorkeling. The sea urchin has an
unusual texture that you can capture with an imprint.

Materials
- 14–16g PMC3 clay
- PMC3 syringe
- 2 3mm and 1 4mm CZs or
  lab-created corundums
- Gold foil
- Vermeil hook
- Vermeil ring
- 20–30 3mm Swarovski crystal
  bicones
- 80–90 2mm vermeil beads
- 150–170 silver-tone seed beads
- Flexible beading wire
- 22-gauge gold-filled wire
- Gold-filled French ear wires
- Sterling silver bail
- Sterling silver crimp beads

Supplies
- Cocktail straw
- Liver of sulfur (optional)

Tools & equipment
- Metal clay basics: balm, fine-tip
  paintbrush, flexible sanding pad,
  plastic mat, playing cards,
  polishing pad, roller, scalpel,
  scissors, small round file,
  tweezers
- Circle-shaped clay cutters:
  ¾ in. (19mm), 1 in. (26mm)
- Sea urchin
- 3 curved drying surfaces
- Kiln setup
- Polishing setup
- Keum-boo setup: agate
  burnishers, gloves, hot plate with
  coil cover (or solid surface)
- Jewelry tools: chainnose pliers,
  crimping pliers, roundnose
  pliers, side cutters

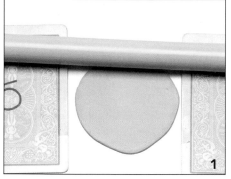

1

2

3

4

5

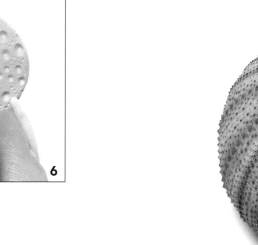

6

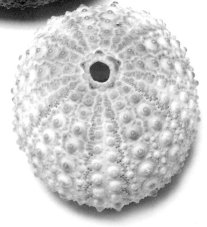

1–2 Roll the clay to the thickness of 5 cards. Use clay cutters to punch out one large disk for the pendant and two small disks for the earrings.

3 Apply extra balm to all three disks and mark the centers of each with a scalpel.

4–5 Place one disk at a time on top of the sea urchin, greased side down, so the center lines up with the hole in the sea urchin. You should be able to see the center of the disk by looking through the bottom of the sea urchin. Imprint each disk by pressing gently with your fingers.

6 Remove each disk from the sea urchin and punch a hole in the center with a cocktail straw.

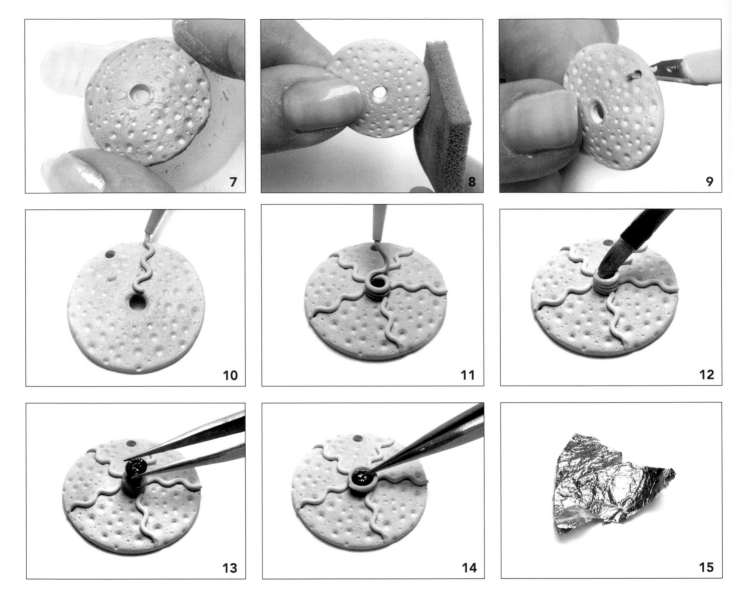

7 Place the disks on the curved drying surfaces to dry completely.

8 Use a flexible sanding pad to sand the outside edges of all three pieces. File the center holes with a round metal file.

9 Using a pencil, mark the locations for the holes on each disk about 3mm from the edge. Insert the tip of the scalpel at a right angle to the piece and rotate the knife without applying pressure. Turn the piece over and repeat so the hole is even on both sides.

10 Add wavy lines of embellishment to the disks with syringe clay.

11 To set the CZ, use a clean paintbrush and water to moisten the area around the center hole. Use syringe clay to create a two- or three-tiered well around the center hole. Don't worry if it isn't perfect!

12 Push out the walls of the well with the paintbrush by placing it in the well and gently moving it in a circular motion. If necessary, the outer walls of the well can be pushed back in gently.

13 Place the CZ upside down and pick it up with the tweezers. Flip it over and place it in the syringe well. Gently push it all the way in with the tweezers, keeping the surface of the CZ horizontal. The edge of the well should be above the CZ's girdle.

14 Repeat steps 11–13 to set a CZ in each of the remaining disks. Dry completely and fire; do not polish.

15 Using scissors, cut triangular pieces of gold foil to fit over the wavy lines on the disks. Heat the hot plate to 800°F (425°C). Place one of the disks on the surface.

Recycle the empty containers from molding compound – they make great curved drying surfaces!

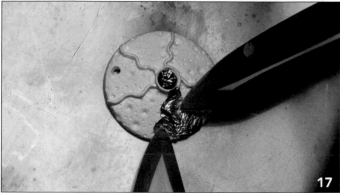

A traditional alternative to the stovetop thermometer is to touch a wooden skewer or chopstick to the metal surface. When it starts to smoke, you know it is at the right temperature for keum-boo.

16–17 Place a piece of foil on the disk. Hold the foil down with one agate burnisher and use the other to burnish the foil onto the piece. Occasionally lift both burnishers from the heat to cool them.

18 Repeat steps 16–17 to add more foil triangles. Complete all three disks this way. Polish the disks and add patina if desired.

To finish the earrings

Using the gold-filled wire, make a wrapped loop on one of the earring charms. String a vermeil bead, a crystal, and a vermeil bead. Link the other end of the wire to an ear wire with a wrapped loop. Repeat for the other earring.

To finish the necklace

Necklace shown is 15 in. (38cm)
Cut a length of flexible beading wire. Attach the bail to the pendant and center it on the wire. String crystals, vermeil beads, and seed beads on both ends until you reach the desired length. Finish by crimping a hook to one end and a ring to the other.

Keum-boo safety

When working with a hot plate, take precautions such as wearing leather gloves and tying long hair back. Don't wear loose clothing and make sure your work area is organized and clear of possible hazards.

Have fun exploring what a touch of gold adds to your silver creations – even older pieces. Keum-boo works best on freshly fired pieces, so refire an older piece before applying gold.

When you finish the keum-boo process, you can achieve some amazing results with a dip – or several – in a liver of sulfur solution. This is your chance to experiment with the unpredictable and beautiful spectrum of colors that can result. For more details on the process of adding a patina, see p. 110.

variations

intermediate

projects

Coil Leaf Charms

I have always thought of grapevine tendrils as nature's little works of art. They add a touch of whimsy to this project.

Materials
- 1½–2g PMC3 clay per charm
- PMC3 syringe
- 16-gauge fine silver wire
- Flexible beading wire
- 1 strand 5–7mm pearls
- 2 in. sterling silver large-link chain
- Sterling silver hook
- 24-gauge sterling silver head pin
- Sterling silver crimp beads
- Sterling silver decorative ear wires

Supplies
- 2 leaves with well-defined veins
- Liver of sulfur (optional)

Tools & equipment
- Metal clay basics: balm, fine-tip paintbrush, flexible sanding pad, plastic mat, playing cards, polishing pad, roller, ruler, scalpel
- Butane torch
- Kiln setup
- Polishing setup
- Jewelry tools: chainnose pliers, crimping pliers, roundnose pliers, side cutters

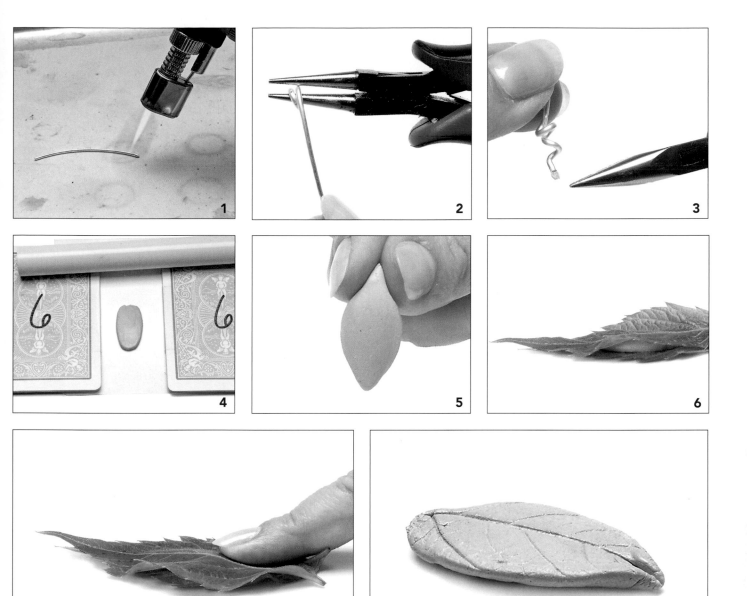

To make a necklace, you'll need about 15 leaf charms. Make two more if you'd like matching earrings.

1–3 To create the wire components, cut lengths of fine silver wire ranging from 1½–3 in. (38–76mm). Use a torch to ball up one end of each wire. Using roundnose and chainnose pliers, start at the balled end of the wire and shape it into a tendril, replicating the twists and turns of grapevine tendrils. Use chainnose pliers to pinch the opposite end of the tendril to flatten it. Make two tendrils for earrings and about fifteen for a necklace.

4–5 Roll an oval of metal clay about ¾ x ⅝ in. (19 x 16mm) to the thickness of 6 cards. Pinch the ends of the oval to make a leaf shape.

6–8 Place the first leaf face up on your work surface. Put the clay on top of the leaf. Place the second leaf on top of the clay, face down, aligning the leaves. Gently press the leaves together with your fingers, applying slightly more pressure at the points to make them a bit thinner than the center of the leaf component. Remove the leaves.

As an alternative, after balling up the end of the wire, you can leave the wire straight and coil it after firing.

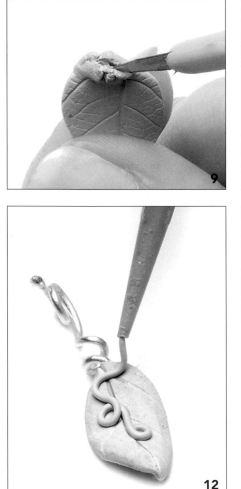

9

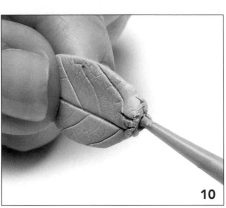

10

11

12

13

To make earrings

Attach leaf charms to ear wires.

To make a necklace

Necklace shown is 16 in. (41cm)
Cut a length of flexible beading wire and string a leaf charm in the center. Alternate stringing pearls and leaf charms on each end, and finish by stringing pearls until you have reached the desired length. Crimp the hook to one side and the length of chain to the other. String a pearl on a head pin and attach it to the end of the chain with a wrapped loop.

9–11 Use a scalpel to carefully cut a small slit at the top of the clay leaf component. Add syringe clay to the inside of the cut. Insert one of the wire tendrils and gently pinch the clay back together. Let dry. Sand if necessary.

12–13 Add syringe clay curves and loops for embellishment as desired.

Make additional charms in the same way, and let all the pieces dry completely. Fire, polish, and add patina if desired.

variations

Your leaf charms can be tiny or large, simply silver or studded with gems. When you're outdoors, look around for plants and trees with leaf forms that intrigue you.

Multistrand Hollow Bracelet

Applying paste to a sculpted cork clay form

One of the underappreciated features of cork clay is that it is easily sculpted. Jewelry pieces made using this technique are lightweight yet have the three-dimensional look of sculpture.

Materials
- PMC3 paste
- 8–10g PMC3
- Flexible beading wire
- 80–90 assorted 3–5mm pearls
- 80–90 2mm fine silver or sterling silver beads
- About 600 2mm filler beads (for inside of hollow cuff)
- Sterling silver toggle clasp
- 6 sterling silver crimp beads

Supplies
- Cork clay
- Clear tape
- Vermiculite
- Liver of sulfur (optional)

Tools & equipment
- Oval bracelet mandrel
- Metal clay basics: balm, burnisher, fine-tip paintbrush, flexible sanding pads, metal file, needle stylus, plastic mat, polishing pad, rolling rectangle, ruler, scalpel
- Kiln setup
- Polishing setup
- Jewelry tools: crimping pliers, side cutters

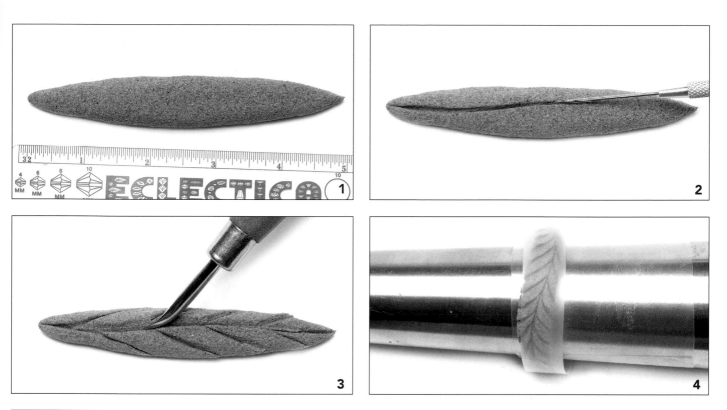

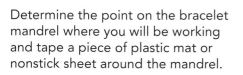

Determine the point on the bracelet mandrel where you will be working and tape a piece of plastic mat or nonstick sheet around the mandrel.

1 Roll a piece of cork clay about 5 in. (13cm) long and ¾ in. (19mm) wide. Taper the ends. Liberally wet the cork shape.

2–3 Use the needle stylus to create deep grooves as shown. Widen the grooves and smooth the edges with a burnisher or a paintbrush handle.

4 Place the cork shape on the mandrel and secure it with tape. Allow to dry thoroughly.

5 Remove the cork shape from the mandrel. Use a pencil to mark where each end is about ⅝ in. (16mm) in diameter. Try not to go past that line as you paint the shape with paste.

6 Apply 12–15 coats of paste, letting each coat dry thoroughly before applying the next. Leave the ends unpainted. Because the thickness of coats may vary, check the weight of the painted piece to tell when you've applied enough paste; it should weigh at least 30g. Let the piece dry completely.

7 Sand with flexible sanding pads, working from coarse to fine grit.

💡 *If the cork clay begins to dry as you're shaping it, mist it lightly with water to extend your working time.*

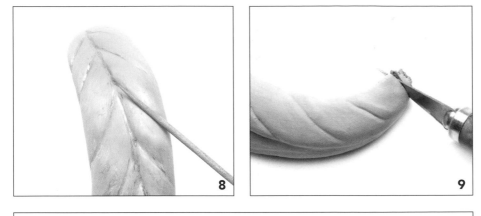

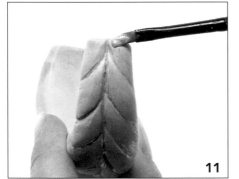

To finish the bracelet

1 Cut six 10-in. (25cm) lengths of flexible beading wire.

2 Separate into three groups of two wires. Crimp each set of two to the toggle ring with a single crimp bead.

3 String 1½–2 in. (38–51mm) of alternating pearls and 2mm silver beads on each of the six strands. Check the fit as you work to determine the right length of beads to string.

4 String a length of 2mm filler beads on each strand equal to the length of the hollow cuff.

5 Slide the beaded strands through the cuff.

6 String 1½–2 in. of pearls and 2mm silver beads on each strand and check the fit.

7 Separate into three groups of two wires each. Crimp one end of each set of two to the toggle bar with a single crimp bead.

8 Use a small round file to smooth the grooves.

9–10 Using a scalpel, cut off the ends of the shape near the point you marked earlier.

11–12 Roll two very thin coils from metal clay. Apply paste and wrap one around each end several times. Dry the piece completely. Fire in vermiculite, polish, and add patina if desired.

Use sculpted cork clay to form focal beads and vessels. As an alternative to the sculpted cuff, make a hollow-core shape with a variety of embellishments – punched shapes, syringe clay, casting grain, and lovely little CZs.

variations

Ocean Waves Ring

These designs evoke the sights and sounds of waves crashing on the beach and the foamy edge of the sea. Applying the freehand syringe work is like using a paintbrush to create a mood; the sea can be stormy or peaceful, depending on the artist's whim.

Materials
- 5–8g PMC3 clay
- PMC3 syringe
- PMC3 paste (optional)
- Casting grain
- 4 x 6mm commercial prong setting
- 4 x 6mm gemstone

Supplies
- Paper or self-stick notes
- Clear tape
- Ring firing form (optional)
- Liver of sulfur (optional)

Tools & equipment
- Metal clay basics: balm, fine-tip paintbrush, flexible sanding pad, full-round sanding stick, plastic mat, playing cards, polishing pad, roller, ruler, scalpel, tissue blade
- Ring mandrel
- Kiln setup
- Polishing setup
- Prong-setting pliers

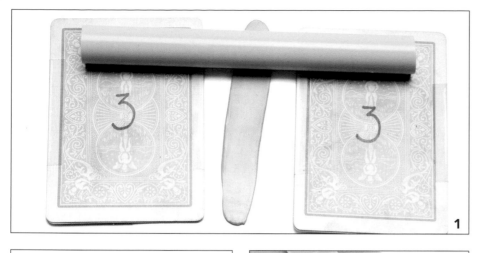

1

2

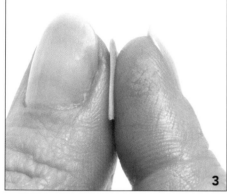

3

4

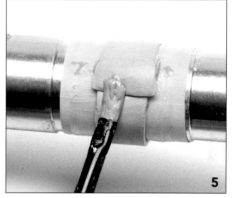

5

Ring Sizing Chart

RING SIZE	BAND LENGTH
Up to size 5	2½ in. (64mm)
Sizes 6–8	2¾ in. (70mm)
Sizes 9–11	3 in. (76mm)
Sizes 12–14	3¼ in. (83mm)

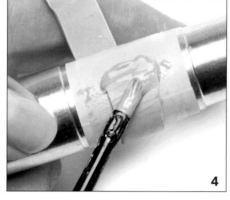

6

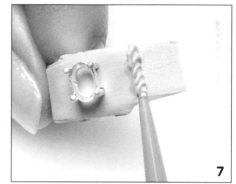

7

Wrap the piece of paper or self-stick note around the point on the mandrel that is two sizes larger than the desired finished size. Wind tape around until the entire piece of paper is covered. Grease the tape liberally.

1–3 Roll the clay to the thickness of 3 cards and about ½ in. (13mm) wide. Use the chart to find the desired length and add an overlap of at least ¼ in. (7mm). Trim with the tissue blade. Pinch each end so it thins slightly.

4–5 Wrap the clay strip around the mandrel. Adhere the seam with paste or syringe clay. Add more paste to smooth the seam.

6 Push the prong setting about 1mm deep in the overlap. Let dry.

7–10 Remove the band from the mandrel and use paste or syringe clay generously to conceal the inside and outside seams. Let the band dry completely.

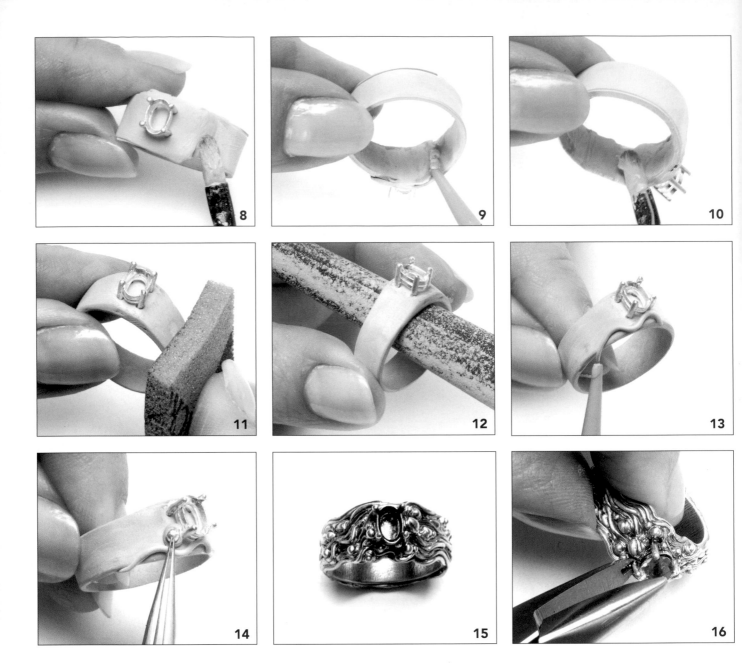

11–12 Use a sanding pad and a full-round sanding stick to sand the band until it is smooth and appears seamless.

13–14 Use syringe clay and casting grain to embellish the band and reinforce the prong setting. Continue until the ring is covered. For a comfortable fit, avoid using large casting grain on the sides or bottom of the band.

15 Dry, fire, polish, and add patina if desired. You may use a ring form to support the ring during firing.

16 Set the gemstone using prong-setting pliers. Hold the pliers so the groove straddles one of the prongs and the dimple in the pliers goes to the opposite prong. With the dimpled part of the pliers, grasp the prong and gently squeeze. The prong should move slightly.

Change the position of the pliers so the groove straddles the opposite prong (the prong that was just moved) and gently squeeze. Repeat this process with the opposite pair of prongs. Check if the stone is secure; if not, repeat the process until it is secure.

When embellishing with syringe, dry your piece between applications to avoid destroying the texture.

Commercial prong settings work well for all kinds of rings, of course, but don't overlook their potential for enhancing stamped pendants and earrings.

variations

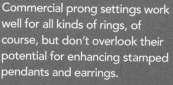

1–2 Rol
6 cards.
on the
with yo
it, and p
Repeat

3–4 Cut
Arrange
trim eac
the piec
edges u

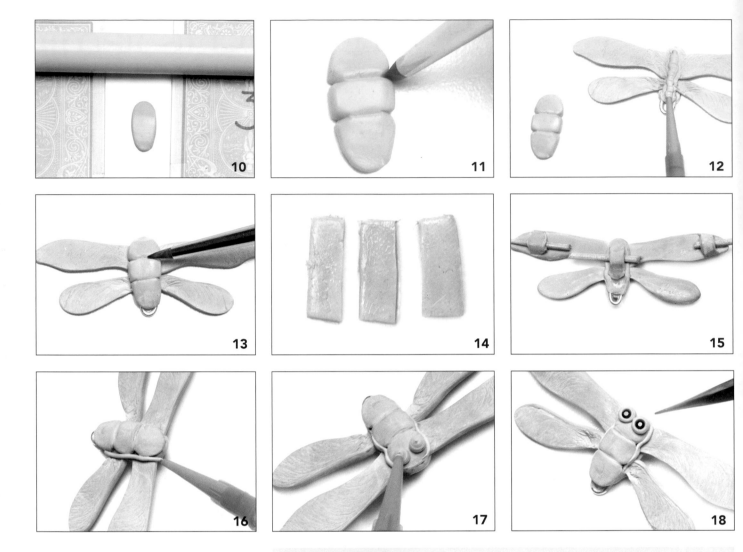

10–13 Roll another piece of clay to the thickness of 3 cards and about ¼ x ⅝ in. Shape it into three segments with a clay shaper. Use syringe clay or paste to adhere it to the body base. Reshape the body if necessary and let dry.

14 Grease three short toothpick segments and set aside. Roll clay to the thickness of 3 cards and cut three bail strips, each ⅛ x ⅜ in. (3 x 10mm).

15 Turn the dragonfly on its back. With syringe clay or paste, attach a bail over each toothpick as shown. Dry the piece and sand smooth.

16 Create an outline around the dragonfly's body with syringe clay.

17–18 Make two blobs for the eyes and set the CZs in them. Fire, polish, and add patina if desired.

To finish the dragonfly and make a necklace

Necklace shown is 16 in. (41cm)

1 Make the dragonfly's tail by stringing several pearls and crystals (separated by daisy spacers) on a head pin. Attach it to the U-shaped wire on the body with a wrapped loop.

2 Create 100–130 head pin components by stringing a pearl or crystal on a head pin and finishing with a wrapped loop.

3 Cut a length of beading wire. Center the dragonfly on the wire through its center bail. String silver beads the length of the dragonfly's wings and then string through the wing bails.

4 String a crystal on each end. String an S-curved tube bead on each end. String another crystal. Create a cluster by alternately stringing head pin components and pearls on both ends. Repeat the process on both ends until you reach the desired length.

5 Crimp one side to the hook and the other to the chain. Link three head pin components to the end of the chain with wrapped loops.

variations

Leaf veins work beautifully to suggest the wings of all kinds of insects. Explore options for the bodies including kiln-safe gems, beaded segments, textured clay, and syringe clay detail.

Sunflower Pendant

Forming a flower's center with brass screen

Sunflowers are cheerful and remind me of the golden days of late summer and fall harvests. Whether you're inspired by sunflowers, daisies, zinnias, or black-eyed susans, this technique will help you capture their beauty in metal clay.

Materials

- 15–20g PMC3 clay
- PMC3 syringe
- PMC3 paste (optional)
- 8–10 2mm CZs or lab-created corundums
- Flexible beading wire
- 120–140 3 x 4mm semiprecious stone rondelles
- 60–100 5–8mm sterling silver tube beads
- 60–80 sterling silver spacer beads
- 2 sterling silver cones
- 2 in. (51mm) sterling silver large-link chain
- 22-gauge half-hard sterling silver wire
- 3 24-gauge sterling silver head pins
- Sterling silver hook
- Sterling silver crimp beads

Supplies

- Solid-brass screen
- Corn husk (optional)
- Cocktail straw
- Small smooth beads
- Liver of sulfur (optional)

Tools & equipment

- Metal clay basics: balm, fine-tip paintbrush, flexible sanding pad, needle stylus, plastic mat, playing cards, polishing pad, roller, ruler, scalpel
- Kiln setup
- Polishing setup
- Jewelry tools: chainnose pliers, crimping pliers, roundnose pliers, side cutters

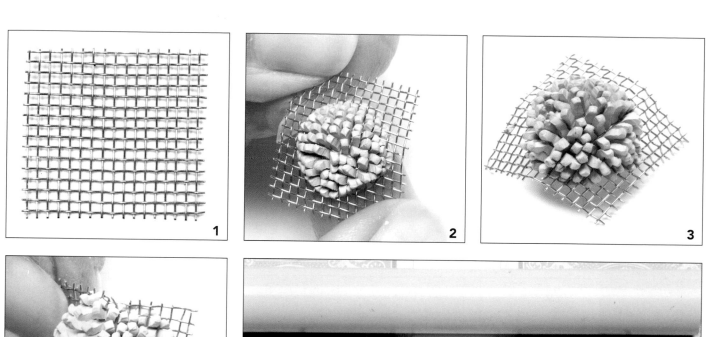

15 Lay the strip over
adhere with paste or
and smooth with a pa
completely, remove t
sand the bail area.

16–17 Embellish the
the petals and the ce
syringe dots and line:
a paintbrush.

18–20 Set the CZs ra
wherever visually ple
making a syringe blo
the CZ in with tweeze

Dry, fire, polish, and
desired.

*The brass screen can be
purchased at a hardware
store. Always start with a
piece of screen that's larger
than the desired finished shape.
The clay spreads as you push it
through. You can always trim the
excess screen after the piece is dry.*

1–3 Cut a piece of brass screen to
1 in. (26mm) square. Roll a piece of
clay into a ball slightly smaller than
½ in. (about 10–12mm) in diameter
and push it through the piece of
screen, but not all the way through.
This will represent the center filled
with seeds. Smooth the back with
your thumb to create a flat surface.
Let the flower center dry completely.

4 Trim the brass screen carefully,
leaving 1–2mm around the clay.

5 Roll a small piece of clay about
½ in. (13mm) long to a thickness of
4 cards. Shape it with your fingers to
resemble a sunflower petal.

6–8 Texture the petal by pressing
it into a piece of corn husk. If you
don't have a corn husk, use the
needle stylus to scribe lines for the
petal texture. Attach the petal to
the flower center with syringe clay.
Push the base of the petal slightly
into the screen.

Create an abundance of texture with the brass-screen technique. What does the pressed clay suggest to you? A hedgehog? An ear of corn? Have fun exploring the possibilities.

variations

Jeweled Prong Setting

Creating a donut pendant with wire prongs

Here's an elegant way to showcase a semiprecious stone donut.
The gems and wire contrast with the donut for extra visual punch.

Materials

- 5–6g PMC3 clay
- PMC3 syringe
- PMC3 paste (optional)
- 16-gauge fine silver wire
- Semiprecious stone donut
- Flexible beading wire
- 3 3mm CZs
- 4mm CZ
- 3 strands 4mm semiprecious stone rondelles (graduated color)
- 280–320 2mm fine silver or sterling silver spacer beads
- 3 22-gauge sterling silver head pins
- Sterling silver hook
- Sterling silver large-link chain
- Sterling silver crimp beads

Supplies

- Cocktail straw
- Paper
- Liver of sulfur (optional)

Tools & equipment

- Metal clay basics: balm, fine-tip paintbrush, flexible sanding pad, plastic mat, playing cards, polishing pad, roller, scalpel
- Tweezers
- Scissors
- Kiln setup
- Polishing setup
- Jewelry tools: chainnose pliers, crimping pliers, roundnose pliers, side cutters
- Flatnose pliers (optional)

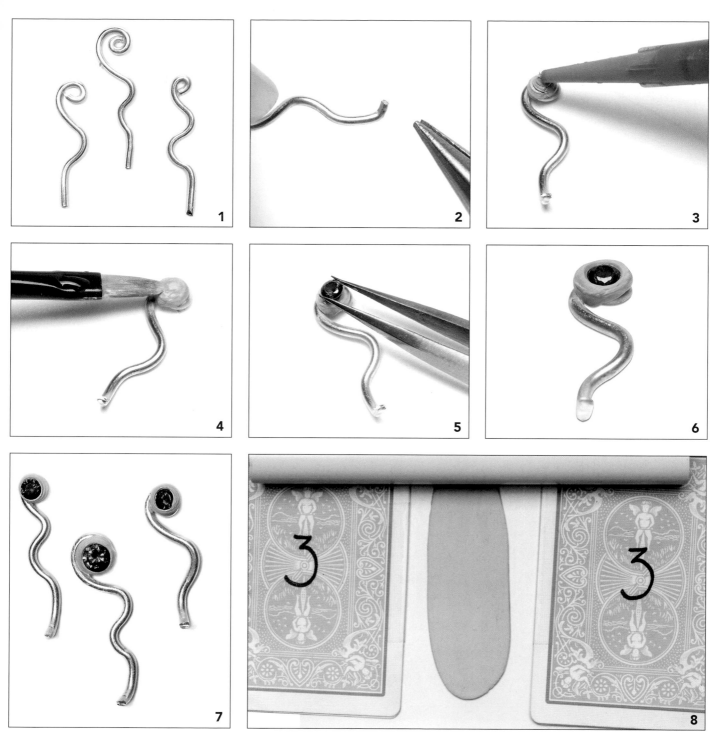

1–2 Using roundnose and chainnose pliers, shape three pieces of wire as shown. Flatten and bend the tip of the straight end of each wire with the chainnose pliers.

3–5 Make a syringe clay blob a bit larger than the CZ being set over the coiled end of one of the wires. Slightly flatten the top of the blob with a paintbrush and push the CZ

in with tweezers. Set two 3mm CZs and one 4mm CZ in this way.

6–7 Be sure the girdle of the stone is below the surface of the syringe clay. Dry the CZ settings completely, then fire.

Create a paper stencil by drawing a circle about twice the width of the donut hole and adding a long

rectangle (see p. 64 for a photo of the stencil). The length of the rectangle should equal or exceed the outer diameter of the donut. Cut out the stencil.

8 Roll the clay to the thickness of 3 cards.

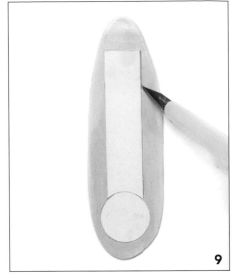

9

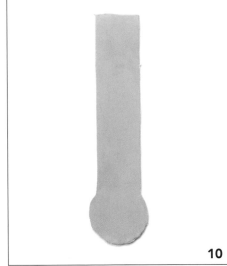

10

11

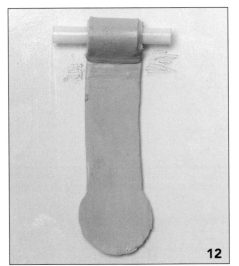

12

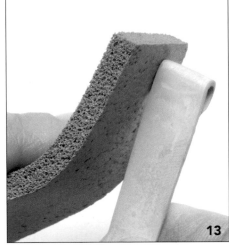

13

When selecting a stone donut for this project, keep in mind the size of the hole needs to be large enough to accommodate the central design element.

9–10 Place the stencil on top of the clay and trace it with a scalpel to cut out the shape.

11–12 Apply paste to the top of the piece. Place a segment of greased straw ½ in. (13mm) from the top and roll the clay over the straw to create the bail. Dry completely.

13 Remove the straw and sand the piece until smooth.

14–15 Embellish the front of the bail with syringe clay and dry completely. Sand the syringe embellishment to flatten it slightly.

16–19 Make a blob in the center of the round section and push each of the prongs into it. Flatten the blob gently with the paintbrush and let dry completely. Make another blob large enough to set the remaining CZ on top of the flattened blob.

15

16

17

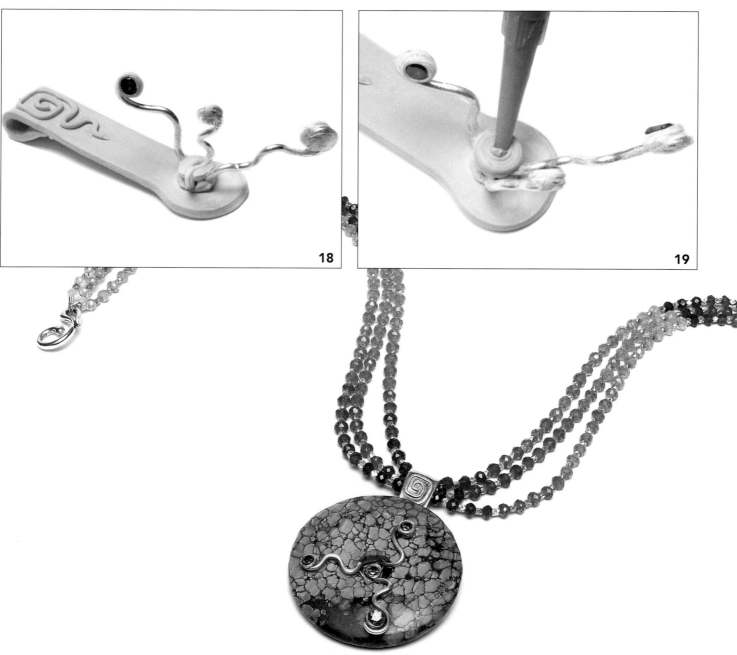

18

19

To finish the necklace

Necklace shown is 16 in. (41cm)
Cut three lengths of flexible beading wire. Center the pendant over all three wires. String an alternating pattern of semiprecious rondelles and 2mm silver beads on each wire until you reach the desired length. Repeat on the other end. Crimp the wires on one end to the hook, and crimp the other wire ends to the large-link chain. String a rondelle on each of the head pins and attach them to the large-link chain with wrapped loops.

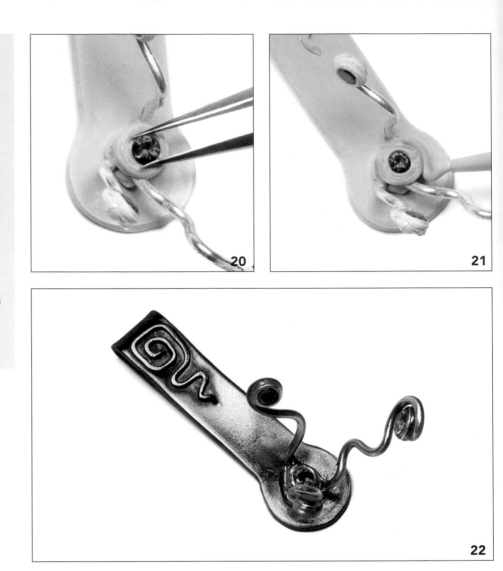

20–22 Set the remaining CZ in the blob and embellish the outside of the setting with syringe clay, decorating and reinforcing the prongs. Dry completely, fire, polish, and add patina if desired.

To set the donut, put the prongs through the opening and bend them over the stone using flatnose or chainnose pliers.

Look around for interesting alternatives to the standard stone donut – try a circle of mother-of-pearl or a Swarovski crystal ring.

Rings allow even more room in the center for experimentation. I introduced leaves into the variations of this project – including leaf-shaped bails and prongs.

variations

Winter Tree Pendant

Trees possess an inherent grace that shines through in every season. I chose a winter tree for this project for its bold, stark lines. The enameling technique I use in this project allows you to achieve an interesting painterly effect to accentuate your tree.

Materials
- PMC+ sheet
- 16–18g PMC3 clay
- PMC3 paste
- PMC3 syringe
- 2 or more colors of lead-free enamels (I used blue and brown)
- Casting grain
- Flexible beading wire
- 70–80 assorted 3–4mm Swarovski round and bicone crystals
- 70–80 2mm fine silver or sterling silver spacer beads
- Sterling silver hook
- 2 in. (51mm) sterling silver large-link chain
- Sterling silver leaf charm
- 24-gauge sterling silver head pin
- Sterling silver crimp beads

Supplies
- Plastic teaspoons
- Small leaves
- Paper
- Cocktail straw
- Liver of sulfur (optional)

Tools & equipment
- Paper punch
- Eyedropper or small spray bottle
- Metal clay basics: balm, fine-tip paintbrush, flexible sanding pad, plastic mat, playing cards, polishing pad, roller, ruler, scalpel
- Scissors
- Kiln setup
- Polishing setup
- Jewelry tools: chainnose pliers, crimping pliers, roundnose pliers, side cutters

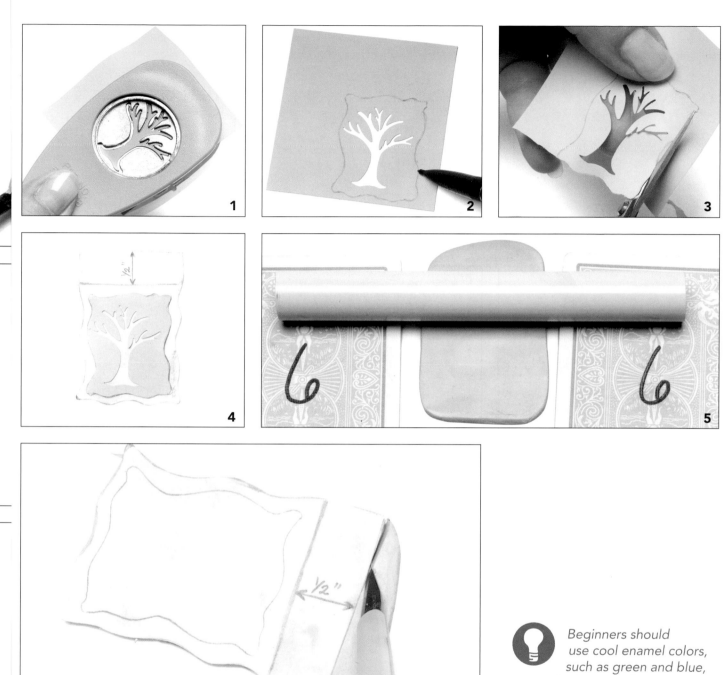

1–3 Using a paper punch, punch a tree image out of the sheet clay. Draw a frame around the negative image with a pencil and cut out the frame.

4 Trace the frame on paper and draw an outer frame, adding about ⅜ in. (10mm) around the edges and ½ in. (13mm) at the top to allow for the rolled bail. Cut out the paper stencil and set the negative image aside to dry.

5–6 Roll clay to the thickness of 6 cards and large enough to accommodate the stencil. Place the paper stencil on the clay and use a scalpel or craft knife to cut around it. Remove the stencil.

Beginners should use cool enamel colors, such as green and blue, for best results. Warm colors like reds and purples are tricky to use because they require precision, both in firing time and order of application. If you're not sure which colors would complement your project, try firing samples on a test piece.

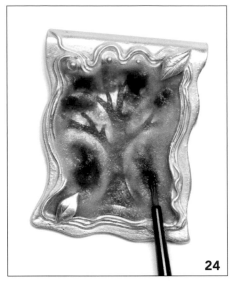

24

25

To finish the necklace

Necklace shown is 16 in. (41cm)
Cut a piece of flexible beading wire. Center the pendant on the wire. String an assortment of crystal beads and silver beads on each end until you reach the desired length. Crimp a hook to one side and the chain to the other. String a 4mm round crystal on the head pin and link it to the leaf charm and the end of the chain with a wrapped loop.

24 To add background color, brush a very thin layer of a light color over the entire surface inside the dam. Add water to help the enamel flow smoothly. Use your paintbrush to add small amounts of the other colors as desired. Fire for 2–3 minutes at 1450°F.

25 Add more layers, if desired, and fire again. Polish and add patina if desired.

variations

Because of metal clay's composition and its ability to take texture, it pairs perfectly with enamels. I enjoy applying and blending enamel colors as if I'm painting with watercolors.

Create new pieces with enameling in mind, or pull out an older creation you'd like to enhance with color. Enamels may open the door to all kinds of colorful possibilities for you.

Amethyst Slice Necklace

Creating wire prongs to set a natural stone

The color and crystal structure of this beautiful amethyst stalactite slice inspired the use of silver flake to complement the texture of the stone.

Materials

- 10–12g PMC3 clay
- PMC3 syringe
- PMC3 paste (optional)
- Silver flake (rough and medium)
- 16-gauge fine silver wire
- 22-gauge half-hard sterling silver wire
- Sterling silver hook and ring clasp
- 20–30 assorted 5–7mm pearls and semiprecious stone beads
- Amethyst stalactite slice

Supplies

- Cocktail straw
- Paper
- Liver of sulfur (optional)

Tools & equipment

- Metal clay basics: balm, fine-tip paintbrush, flexible sanding pad, plastic mat, playing cards, polishing pad, roller, scalpel
- Tweezers
- Scissors
- Kiln setup
- Polishing setup
- Jewelry tools: chainnose pliers, roundnose pliers, side cutters

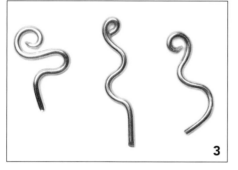

1

2

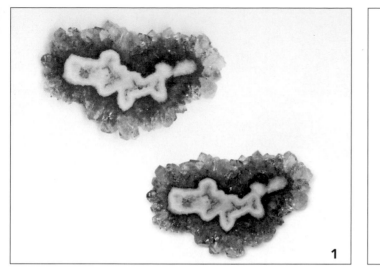

3

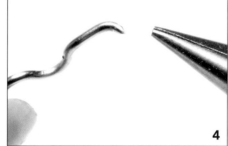

4

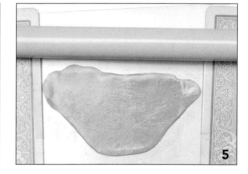

5

6

7

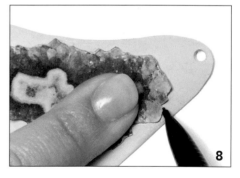

8

1–2 Make a photocopy of the stone, enlarging it to 112% to allow for clay shrinkage, then design the pendant around the photocopy. Use a pencil to draw an outline around the stone. Include at least three spots for prongs and two spots for connector holes. Cut out the design with scissors.

3–4 Use chainnose pliers to shape short lengths of wire for the prongs. Pinch the tip of the straight end of each prong to flatten it.

5–7 Roll clay to the thickness of 4 cards and large enough to

accommodate the pattern. Trace the outline of the pattern onto the clay with a scalpel. Use a cocktail straw to punch out the connector holes at the top of the pendant. Let dry.

8 In pencil, outline the photocopy of the stone on the clay base.

When selecting a stone for this piece, make sure the crystals along the edge are not too fragile.

9

10

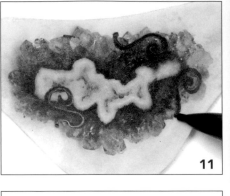
11

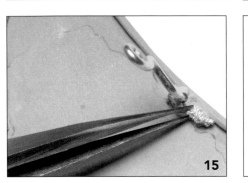
12

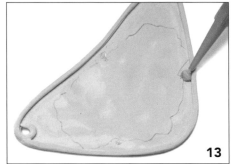
13

14

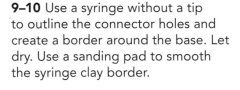
15

16

17

9–10 Use a syringe without a tip to outline the connector holes and create a border around the base. Let dry. Use a sanding pad to smooth the syringe clay border.

11–12 Push the tip of the pencil through the pattern to mark the points where the prongs will attach to the base.

13–14 Make syringe blobs at each point and push the prongs into

place. Consider the position of the stone and keep the syringe clay blobs clear of that area.

15–16 Use syringe clay or paste to adhere the silver flakes to the base. Take care to avoid the area within the stone outline. Let dry, then fire, polish, and add patina if desired.

17 Position the stone. Carefully bend the prongs over it to secure.

To finish the necklace

Necklace shown is 17 in. (43cm)
Make links with pearls and semiprecious stones by stringing them on a wire and making a wrapped loop on each end. Alternate pearls and gemstones, and connect the links before you complete the wraps. Make two chains equal to about half your desired length. Connect one end of each chain to each side of the pendant. Connect a hook to one remaining end and the ring to the other.

Look to your focal stone for ideas on shaping the base and placing the prongs.

These pendants hold iridized drusies. I studied the bends and crevices as I designed prong settings for them. The ring showcases a half-drilled mabe pearl held by a hidden wire prong.

variations

advanced

projects

Art Deco Setting

In this project, you'll create a simple setting for a large CZ that mimics the look of a traditional stone setting. One of the advantages of this technique is that it can be used to set unusually shaped stones.

Materials
- 12g PMC3 clay
- PMC3 syringe
- PMC3 paste (optional)
- 14mm CZ
- 25–35 assorted 3–4mm bicone and round crystals
- 22-gauge half-hard sterling silver wire
- Sterling silver toggle clasp
- 10 6–8mm (outside diameter) sterling silver jump rings

Supplies
- Self-stick notes
- Clear tape
- Liver of sulfur (optional)

Tools & equipment
- Metal clay basics: balm, files, fine-tip paintbrush, flexible sanding pad, full-round sanding stick, needle stylus, plastic mat, playing cards, polishing pad, roller, ruler, scalpel

- Stamp
- 10–12mm round clay cutter
- Ring mandrel
- Kiln setup
- Polishing setup
- Jewelry tools: chainnose pliers, roundnose pliers, side cutters

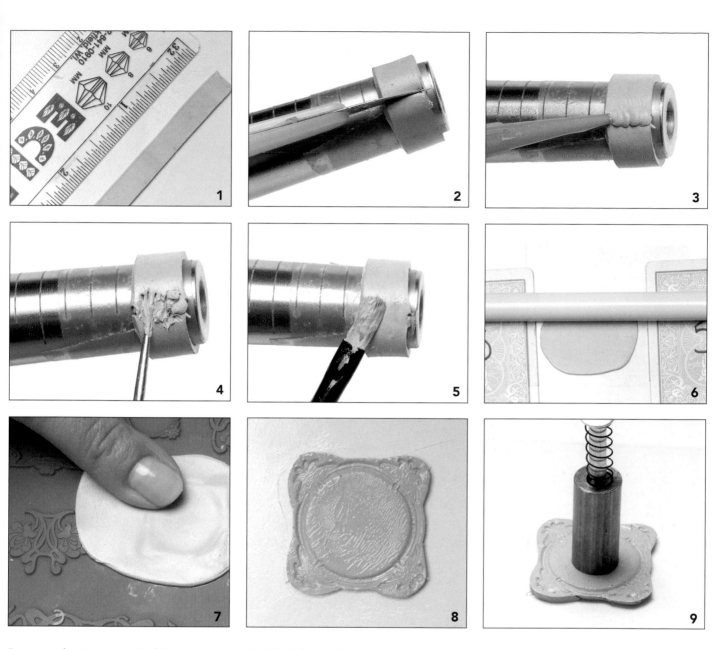

Prepare the ring mandrel by wrapping a self-stick note around the mandrel at size 1, then wrap a piece of clear tape all the way around the paper. Grease the tape.

1–2 Roll the clay to the thickness of 4 cards into a strip at least 2 x ¼ in. (51 x 7mm). Wrap the strip around the mandrel and cut off extra clay. Adhere the seam with syringe clay and let dry.

3–5 Reinforce the seam with syringe clay or paste. Drag the needle stylus across the seam several times to mix the clay and strengthen the bond. Smooth the seam with the paintbrush. Remove the band from the mandrel to fill and smooth the inside seam. Let dry.

6–7 Roll a piece of clay to the thickness of 5 cards and large enough to cover the stamp. Grease the clay, place it on the stamp, and roll to 4 cards thick (or press the clay onto the stamp with your fingers).

8–9 Remove the clay from the stamp and cut out the base component. Punch a hole in the center using a clay cutter. Let dry.

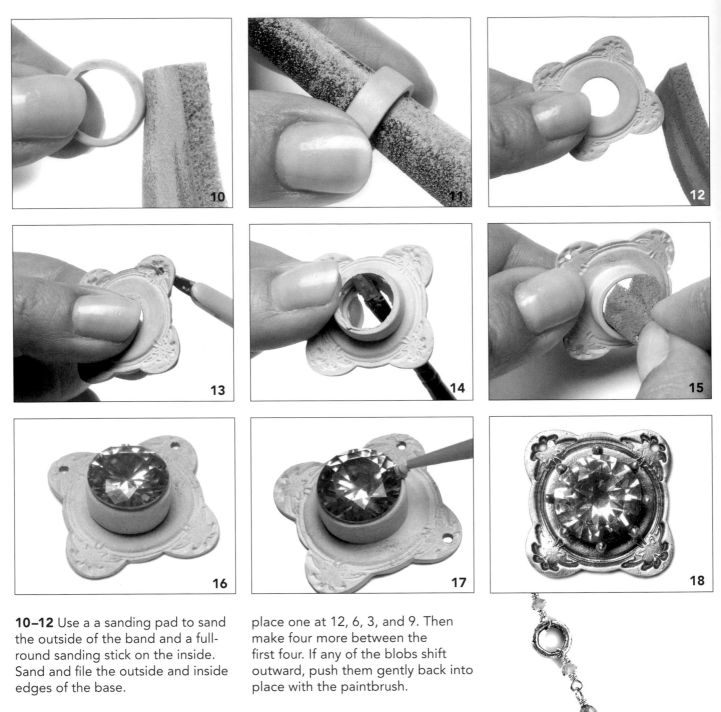

10–12 Use a a sanding pad to sand the outside of the band and a full-round sanding stick on the inside. Sand and file the outside and inside edges of the base.

13 Use a scalpel to create two connecting holes.

14–16 With syringe clay or paste, adhere the band to the base, fill any gaps, and smooth with the paintbrush. Let dry completely. Use the full-round sanding stick or a rolled sanding pad to smooth the opening. To set the CZ, moisten the top edge of the setting with a paintbrush and place the CZ on top.

17 Create blobs of equal size with syringe clay. As if on a clock face,

place one at 12, 6, 3, and 9. Then make four more between the first four. If any of the blobs shift outward, push them gently back into place with the paintbrush.

18 Dry, fire, polish, and add patina if desired.

To finish the necklace

Necklace shown is 16 in. (41cm)
Make links with crystals and jump rings by stringing them on a wire and making a wrapped loop on each end. Alternate bicones, rounds, and jump rings, and connect the links before you complete the wraps. Make two chains equal to about half the desired length. Connect one end of each chain to each side of the pendant. Connect the toggle bar to one remaining end and the toggle ring to the other.

variations

Your gem settings will look polished and professional with this technique. Prongs can be created in a number of ways – in the pendant below, I used small leaf shapes stamped from sheet clay along with syringe clay.

Vine Bead Cage

Using cork clay to create a bead with a secret treasure

This project features a hidden treasure: a bead within a bead. Use cork clay to hide a bit of sparkle inside a sophisticated silver cage built of syringe clay.

Materials
- 25g PMC3 clay
- PMC3 syringe
- PMC3 paste (optional)
- 8mm round CZ bead
- Flexible beading wire
- 3 strands of pearls
- 2mm fine silver or sterling silver beads
- Sterling silver hook
- 2 in. (51mm) sterling silver large-link chain
- Sterling silver head pin
- 2 3mm sterling silver daisy spacers
- Sterling silver crimp beads
- 2 sterling silver crimp covers

Supplies
- Cork clay
- Round toothpicks
- Vermiculite
- Liver of sulfur (optional)

Tools & equipment
- Metal clay basics: balm, fine-tip paintbrush, needle stylus, plastic mat, polishing pad, rolling rectangle, ruler
- Kiln setup
- Polishing setup
- Jewelry tools: chainnose pliers, crimping pliers, roundnose pliers, side cutters

 Because it will be fired inside the bead cage, make sure the round treasure bead you choose for this project is a kiln-ready CZ or lab-created stone.

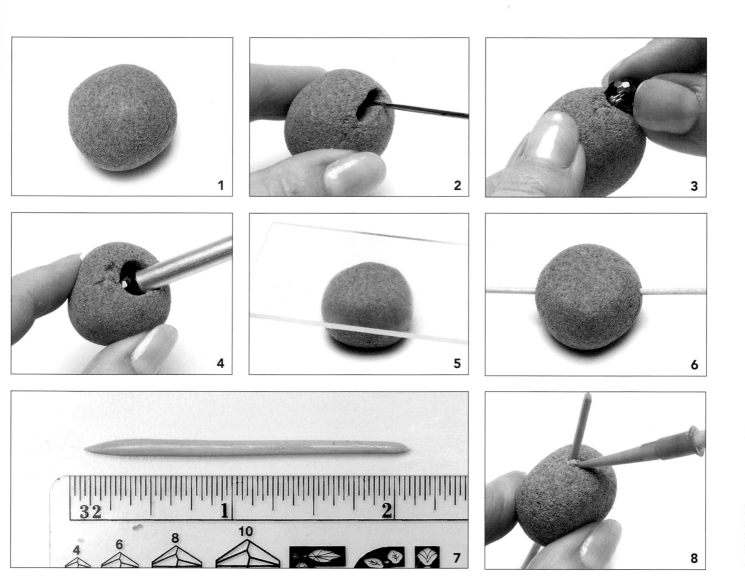

1–2 Create a 1-in. (26mm) ball out of cork clay. Using a needle stylus, cut an opening in the cork clay as shown. The opening needs to be just a bit larger than the CZ bead.

3–4 Insert the bead in the opening and bury it deep enough so you're able to close the opening entirely.

5–6 Shape the cork clay until it's round again and use a rolling rectangle to slightly flatten the top and bottom. Insert a toothpick in each side of the cork clay form.

7–8 Roll a small piece of metal clay to 2 in. (51mm) and about ⅛ in. (3mm) diameter. You will coil this piece into a spiral cap around the toothpick. Add syringe clay around the opening where you will start the spiral.

9

10

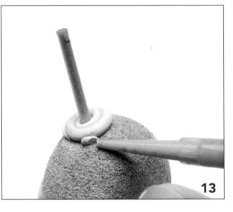

11

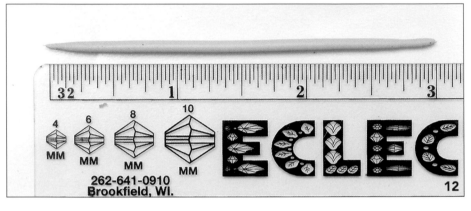

12

13

14

15

16

9–11 As you make the spiral, add syringe clay between the coils. Use the paintbrush to smooth the spiral. Repeat to make another spiral cap around the opposite opening.

12–15 Roll a 3-in. (76mm) coil and attach it with syringe clay, positioning it diagonally across the cork clay from the top cap to the bottom cap. Repeat on the other side of the form.

16 Roll several more coils and attach them to create a network of curving vines. Use syringe clay or paste at the points where they touch.

17–19 To make the leaf shapes that are interspersed among the vines, roll about 1g of clay into a ball. Flatten and shape it with your fingers into a leaf shape about ½ in. (13mm) long. Use the needle stylus to scribe deep veins. Smooth the leaf shape with a clean, moist brush.

Repeat to make more leaf shapes ranging from ¼–½ in. (7–13mm). My bead cage incorporates about 25 leaves of slightly different sizes.

20–21 Attach the leaves to the vine network as desired until there are no openings bigger than the CZ bead. You can also add more vines to fill gaps. Let dry.

Examine all the joins. Reinforce with syringe clay or paste if necessary. Let dry completely, then fire in vermiculite, polish, and add patina if desired.

To finish the necklace

Necklace shown is 17 in. (43cm)
1 Cut six 10-in. (25cm) pieces of flexible beading wire.

2 String three pieces of flexible beading wire through a daisy spacer and a crimp. Crimp. Trim the wire and cover the crimp with a crimp cover.

3 Thread the other ends of the wires through a large opening in the bead and then through one of the side holes. Position the crimped end so the daisy spacer rests against the inside of the hole.

4 String all three strands with pearls or a combination of pearls and 2mm silver beads.

5 Crimp the ends of the three strands to the hook.

6 Repeat steps 2–5 for the other end, substituting the large-link chain for the hook.

7 String a pearl on a head pin and link it to the chain with a wrapped loop.

variations

A bead cage can take forms other than round – try an oval, a square, or a triangle shape, for example. The vines and leaves can encircle and hold pretty treasures such as a crystal, a lampworked bead, porcelain, or dichroic glass.

Endless Link Bracelet

Chain is a wonderful element of jewelry design. This linking technique will enable you to create unique and versatile chain to stand on its own or enhance any project.

Materials
- 20–25g PMC3 clay
- PMC3 syringe
- Art Clay oil paste
- 16-gauge fine silver wire

Supplies
- Self-stick notes
- Clear tape
- Vermiculite
- Liver of sulfur (optional)

Tools & equipment
- Mandrel (I used a ⅝ in./16mm oval clay cutter)
- Metal clay basics: balm, files, fine-tip paintbrush, flexible sanding pad, full-round sanding stick, plastic mat, playing cards, polishing pad, roller, rolling rectangle, ruler, scalpel
- Round clay cutters: ¾ in. (19mm), ⅝ in. (16mm), ⅜ in. (10mm)
- Butane torch
- Kiln setup
- Polishing setup
- Jewelry tools: chainnose pliers, side cutters

Nearly any item can be used as a mandrel. Try clay cutters, square dowel rods, markers, or brush handles, or you can make your own mandrels out of wood or polymer clay.

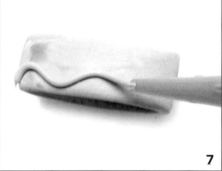

1–2 The mandrel I used for this project was an oval clay cutter. Wrap the mandrel with a self-stick note, then wrap tape around the entire note. Grease the tape.

3 Roll clay to the thickness of 4 cards. Cut to create a strip 2 x 3/8 in. (51 x 10mm).

4–6 Wrap the clay over the mandrel and add syringe clay or paste at the seam. Smooth with the paintbrush and let dry completely. Sand to smooth the link.

7 Embellish both sides of the oval link with syringe clay. Let dry completely.

8 Lightly sand the top of the embellishment with a sanding pad to flatten it slightly.

Repeat steps 1–8 until you have the desired number of oval links (my bracelet has eight). Fire the links, or set aside to fire with additional components.

variations

Apply your skill in shaping metal clay links to making bails and connecting larger components.

As an advanced artisan, you'll be able to combine techniques to build your own metal clay sampler. My kinetic pendant at left combines sea urchin texturing, keum-boo, and detailed syringe work — all held in place with an embellished endless link.

Bezeled Sand Dollar

I have always been fascinated by the ocean. It's like another world, full of mystery and peace. I hope that you enjoy creating your own talisman of the sea.

Materials

- 10–12g PMC3 clay
- PMC3 syringe
- Art Clay oil paste
- Casting grain
- Fine silver bezel strip to fit circumference of fossil (about 5 in./13cm)
- 4 x 6mm oval CZ
- Fossilized sand dollar (mine is about 1¼ in./32mm wide)
- Flexible beading wire
- Strand 5 x 8mm faceted pearls
- 10 3–4mm pearls
- 2 in. (51mm) sterling silver large-link chain
- Sterling silver hook clasp
- 20-gauge fine silver wire, 1 in. (26mm)
- 10 26-gauge decorative sterling silver head pins
- Sterling silver crimp beads

Supplies

- Two-part molding compound
- Liver of sulfur (optional)
- Cork clay
- Twig for molding
- E6000 adhesive (optional)

Tools & equipment

- Butane torch
- Metal clay basics: balm, burnisher, fine-tip paintbrush, flexible sanding pads, polishing pad, roller, rolling rectangle, plastic mat, playing cards, scalpel
- Tweezers
- Scissors
- Kiln setup
- Polishing setup
- Jewelry tools: chainnose pliers, crimping pliers, roundnose pliers, side cutters

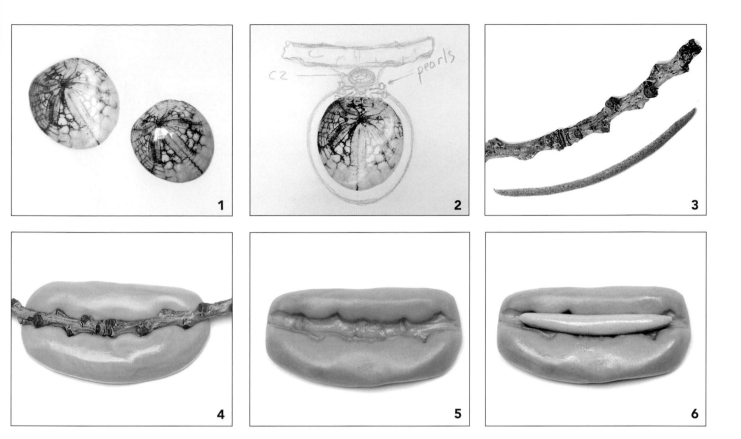

1–2 Make a photocopy of the cabochon, enlarging it to 112% to allow for shrinkage. Design the pendant around the photocopy and cut around the outline of the pattern with scissors.

3 Use the rolling rectangle to roll the cork clay to the length of the bail tube or longer, with a diameter slightly smaller than the twig. The cork clay will create the hollow part of the bail tube.

4–5 Mix enough two-part molding compound for the twig impression. Press the twig into the compound and let the mold set. Remove the twig from the mold. You'll use the mold to make a half-round shape for the bail tube.

6 Roll the metal clay to fill the mold.

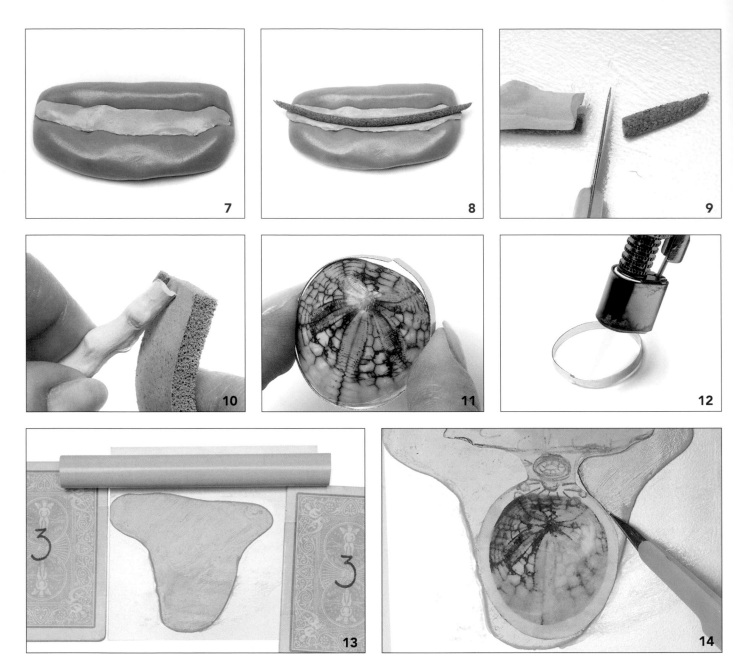

7–8 Use your fingers to gently press clay into every part of the mold. Press the cork clay into the metal clay to create a hollow bail tube. Be careful not to push it too close to the edges. Let the assembly dry.

9–10 Remove the clay from the mold and trim the ends with the scalpel. Sand the bail tube to smooth.

11–12 Wrap the bezel strip around the cabochon. Trim the ends with scissors so they meet in a straight line with no gap. Use the torch to fuse the ends together. (When the fine silver wire is heated, it will join without solder.)

13–15 Roll clay to the thickness of 3 cards and large enough to accommodate your pattern. Place the pattern on top of the clay and cut out the shape by tracing the outline with the scalpel.

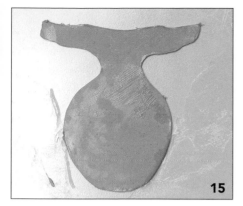

15

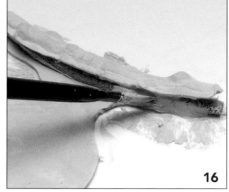

16

17

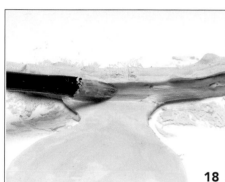

18

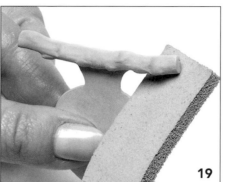

19

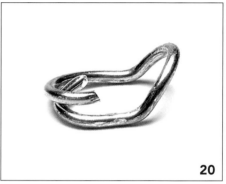

20

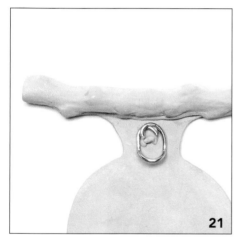

21

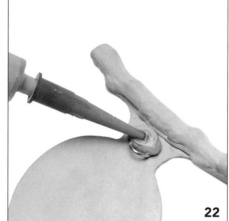

22

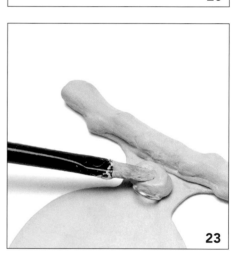

23

16–19 Apply paste to the back of the bail tube, the cork clay, and the base. Using the paintbrush, shape the moist base around the cork clay to meet the dry bail tube. Use paste to adhere the components and fill the seam. Smooth with the brush and let dry completely. Sand the entire piece.

20–21 Cut and shape the wire component as shown, making it wide enough to frame the CZ. Center it on the base, below the bail. Later you'll add pearls on wrapped loops to this wire (see *To finish the necklace*, p. 100, for beading instructions).

22–23 Create a large oval blob with syringe clay, covering the top of the wire component but leaving the loop exposed. This will form the setting for the CZ. Smooth with the paintbrush.

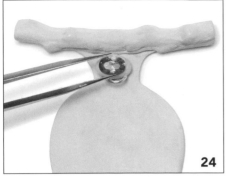

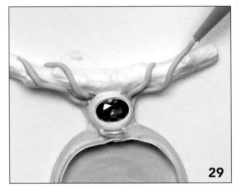

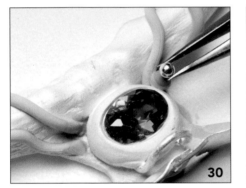

24–25 Set the CZ in the syringe blob, pushing the girdle of the stone below the surface of the clay. Let dry completely. Fire the assembly.

26–27 Paint the front of the base with oil paste and position the bezel. Let dry. If there are any gaps between the bezel and the pendant base, fill them with oil paste.

28–30 Add syringe clay and casting grain embellishments around the bezel, the bail tube, and the CZ.

31 Fire, polish, and add patina.

32 Secure the stone with E6000 adhesive, if desired. Push the bezel strip over the stone with a bezel pusher or a burnisher.

To finish the necklace

Necklace shown is 16 in. (41cm)
1 String several small pearls on decorative head pins and link them to the wire loop below the CZ with wrapped loops.

2 Cut a length of flexible beading wire and center the pendant on the wire. String pearls on each end until you reach the desired length. Crimp one end to the hook and the other to the large-link chain. String a pearl on a head pin and link it to the end of the chain with a wrapped loop.

The ability to make a bezel allows you to use a broad variety of cabochons in your work. Because the cabochon is added after firing, you don't need to be concerned about whether it is kiln-safe.

Add some accent gems if you choose, or incorporate casting grain, syringe work, and wrapped-loop beads or pearls.

materials &

tools

Materials and Tools

paste

oil paste

lump clay

PMC Sheet

sheet clay

SINGLE USE ON

syringe clay

METAL CLAY BASICS

Metal clay is a revolutionary, easy-to-form material that has tremendous potential for the craft artisan. In its moist form, small metal particles are suspended in an organic binder. When fired, the binder burns away, leaving solid metal.

Silver metal clay, which is used for all the projects in this book, is available in four forms: lump clay, syringe clay, paste, and sheet clay. Two brands are currently sold – **Precious Metal Clay** (PMC) and **Art Clay**. Products in both lines have similar properties and come with complete firing directions.

Lump clay can be rolled into sheets or coils, textured, sculpted, or shaped by hand. Kiln-safe cubic zirconia (CZs) and lab-created gemstones can be set in it and safely fired. Lump clay contains a low proportion of water and can dry out quickly. Keep it moist by periodically misting it with water; cover unused clay with plastic wrap.

Syringe clay is watered-down metal clay in a syringe applicator. Use syringe clay to adhere pieces together, to set stones and casting grain, and to create bails, lines, dots, spirals, and other shapes. Its possibilities are limitless, particularly if you have a steady hand.

Paste has the consistency of thick paint. Paste can be purchased, or you can make your own by adding a bit of water to leftover bits of unfired metal clay and clay dust. Paste can be painted onto bisque beads, organic items, or cork clay. Thinned paste, often called "slip," is used to join pieces of unfired clay.

Sheet clay is oil-based and doesn't dry out as you work. It can be precisely folded like paper, cut with scissors, or punched with paper punches to form intricate shapes. Sheet clay does not stick to itself; use paste or Elmer's glue to laminate sheet clay into a thicker sheet.

The projects call for specific types of metal clay. **PMC3** has a lower firing temperature and shrinks less than PMC Standard and PMC+. It is the best product to use for making rings because it is denser after firing and can withstand heavy wear. PMC3 products have a shrinkage rate of about 12%, the same as PMC+ sheet. You can combine PMC3 with PMC+ if you fire the finished piece at the PMC+ temperature.

PMC3 syringe clay comes with one tip that you apply tightly before use. If you find that the opening is too small, cut off the tip with a scalpel. Store syringe clay with the tip resting in water to prevent it from drying out.

PMC+ Sheet is an oil-based product that doesn't contain water, so it remains workable much longer than other forms of PMC. PMC+ is not

a low-fire product: When you combine PMC+ with PMC3, you must use the higher temperature recommended for PMC+. The shrinkage rate of PMC+ is 10–12%.

Art Clay Oil Paste is used to adhere pieces together and to make repairs. It is especially effective when one or both of the pieces has been fired, or when attaching a fine silver component such as a bezel or wire.

Recycle extra clay while it's fresh for the best paste. Put leftovers in an airtight glass or plastic container, add a little water, and in a few hours you'll have paste. If it seems too thin, leave the container open and let some water evaporate. Don't mix different types of clay, and label the container of paste.

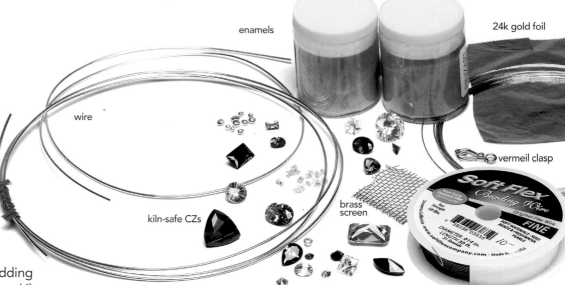

enamels

24k gold foil

wire

kiln-safe CZs

vermeil clasp

brass
screen

flexible beading wire

Some of the additional materials you'll use to complete your metal clay jewelry include silver wire, findings, and flexible beading wire – not to mention a stash of beautiful beads, pearls, and crystals!

Use **fine silver wire** when adding wire to silver clay before firing. Like the clay, it is pure silver and doesn't develop firescale in the kiln. But because it is pure, it's also softer than sterling silver; using a tumbler or magnetic polisher to harden the piece after firing is a good idea.

For wire components added *after* firing, use **sterling silver wire** because of its greater durability. For the same reason, and also because they are readily available, I use sterling silver spacers, crimps, and clasps.

When a design calls for gold, like the sea urchin set made with the keum-boo technique, I use components that are either gold-filled or vermeil (pronounced *vermay*).

Gold-filled refers to base metal components that are plated with karat gold in a fusing process. **Vermeil** refers to sterling silver components that are heavily electroplated with gold. For the keum-boo process itself, choose **genuine karat gold foil**, not gold leaf, which is too thin. Gold foil is available from sources that sell jewelry and metal clay supplies.

Use fine silver **casting grain** to add detail to silver clay pieces. You can make your own by balling up small pieces of fine silver wire with a torch – it's a great use for small bits of scrap wire, and you can control the size

of the resulting grain. **Silver flake** is another embellishment; it's available in various sizes of flakes.

When choosing a **CZ** or **lab-grown corundum** that will be fired in a metal clay component, check that it is identified as kiln-safe – your assurance that it can withstand firing without fracturing or cracking.

For enameling, I recommend using **lead-free enamels** and starting with cool colors if you're a beginner. You'll find a wide range of colors available from art, ceramics, and enameling supply distributors.

These basic clay-shaping tools are the "must-haves" for nearly every metal clay project. Keep them handy!

Any surface that touches metal clay must be lightly greased. This includes the work mat, roller, and any miscellaneous tools such as straws for making bails. A natural hand **balm** or **olive oil** works well.

Use a **ball stylus** to create textures or to push down on clay in place of your finger to avoid leaving a fingerprint.

Clay shaper tools are available with differently shaped tips, and are used to shape clay or blend seams.

Use a **fine-tip paintbrush** to apply slip. Always keep a **small cup of water** handy. Moisten the brush for shaping and smoothing. Use it dry to brush clay debris off sanded pieces.

Use a **needle stylus** to make or mark holes. It also works well for signing the back of your pieces before firing. In a pinch, use a sharp pencil.

A must for wiping brushes, **paper towels** are also used to wick away excess water if you accidentally put too much on your piece. Simply touch a corner of the towel to the wet portion and watch the water soak upward; avoid wiping the wet piece.

Create **plastic work mats** by cutting apart clear report covers or flexible Teflon baking sheets. Lightly grease the mat before working on it. If the mat becomes scored, change to a new mat to avoid marring your work.

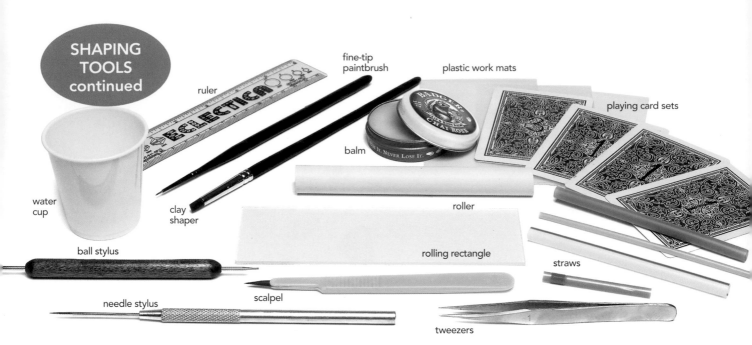

ruler

fine-tip paintbrush

plastic work mats

playing card sets

balm

roller

water cup

clay shaper

rolling rectangle

straws

ball stylus

needle stylus

scalpel

tweezers

Use **playing cards** to control the thickness of rolled clay. Tape cards together to make sets of 2, 3, 4, 5, and 6. In some cases you may want a single-card thickness.

Used to smoothly flatten metal clay to a specific thickness, a **roller** may be a length of PVC pipe, an acrylic rod, or a brayer. Always grease the roller lightly before use.

A **rolling rectangle** is a piece of clear plastic used to roll clay into smooth, uniform cylinders or coils.

Use a small, clear **ruler** that measures millimeters and inches. Beads are usually sized in millimeters.

I like to use a **scalpel** for cutting clay and making small holes. A craft knife can be used as well.

Use narrow **stir or cocktail straws** to create dainty bails, and **drinking straws** for larger bails. Straws also can be used to punch holes in clay.

Use **tweezers** to pick up and set CZs and casting grain, and to remove leaves and stems after imprinting them. They are also helpful for removing polished pieces from a magnetic polisher.

ABRASIVE TOOLS

flexible sanding pads

small metal files

emery board

full-round sanding stick

An **emery board** is handy for filing flat edges and surfaces. Use **flexible sanding pads** to smooth dimensional pieces such as vessels, beads, and rings.

Full- and half-round sanding sticks are used to sand the inside of curved surfaces such as rings. They are available in different grits and are usually are sold in sets.

Use **metal files** to file irregularly shaped pieces or to get into crevices that an emery board or flexible sanding pad just can't reach. I suggest you keep two sets handy: small and extra-small.

FINISHING PRODUCTS AND TOOLS

polishing pads

pointed-tip agate burnisher

polishing cloth

knife-shaped agate burnisher

wire brush

burnisher

liver of sulfur

Agate burnishers are used to give a bright polish to the high spots on your fired piece. They're also used in the keum-boo process to tack and burnish gold foil onto fired metal clay. A burnisher also can be used as a bezel pusher.

Liver of sulfur – smelly but nontoxic – gives a patina or an antique finish to fired pieces. It's economical to buy in lump form; mix a small piece or two with warm water as needed.

Polishing pads remove most of the liver of sulfur, leaving color only in the low spots of the piece. **Polishing**

cloths give a final shine to any fired piece, whether a patina has been applied or not. No polishing compound is necessary.

If you don't have access to a tumbler or magnetic polisher, use a **wire brush** to polish fired pieces.

PROJECT-SPECIFIC TOOLS

bracelet and ring mandrels

cork clay on wood skewer and toothpicks

clay cutters and paper punch

spray bottle

assortment of texture tools

bisque bead forms

ring form

molding compound

To add texture to clay, use **acrylic texture sheets, brass plates, and rubber stamp mats**.

Bisque beads are fired, unglazed porcelain beads that are used as cores for metal clay beads. They do not burn away during firing.

Punch shapes out of clay with **clay cutters** and **paper punches**.

Cork clay is a moldable substance used to create hollow-form pieces; the cork burns away during firing.

Mandrels are used for forming rings and bracelets, and for holding pieces as you work on them.

Ring forms or pellets retain the shape and size of a ring while it is being fired; they are not reusable.

Use a small **spray bottle** or an eyedropper to hydrate clay and to add water to enamels.

Mix equal amounts of **two-part molding compound** until you get a uniform color, then impress an object to get a reusable mold.

Toothpicks or wood skewers are handy for punching holes or for forming small bails. Skewers are also helpful for holding cork clay forms for hollow beads and vessels.

JEWELRY TOOLS

The jaws of **chainnose pliers** taper to a fine point. This offers a lot of control and precision for bending wire into right angles and opening jump rings and plain loops. These pliers also are used with roundnose pliers to make wrapped loops (see sidebar, below right).

Crimping pliers have two sets of grooves in their jaws so you can close and then fold crimp beads around flexible beading wire. This detail gives a professional finish to necklace and bracelet ends (see sidebar below).

Flatnose pliers have blunt tips that are wider than those of chainnose pliers. Use these to turn spirals out of

crimping pliers

roundnose pliers

prong-setting pliers

flatnose pliers

small, sharp scissors

side cutters

chainnose pliers

wire. **Roundnose pliers** are essential for shaping wire into curves and creating plain and wrapped loops. Sheet clay can be cut with small, sharp

scissors. The small, angled blades of **side cutters** cut wire with accuracy. **Prong-setting pliers** are used to set CZs in commercial settings.

Crimping

To crimp half a clasp to a necklace or bracelet end, position the crimp bead in the notch closest to the crimping pliers' handle **[a]**. Separate the wires and firmly squeeze the crimp to close it **[b]**.

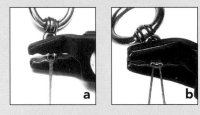

Move the crimp into the notch at the pliers' tip. Squeeze the crimp bead, folding it in half at the indentation **[c]**. Tug the clasp to make sure the folded crimp is secure **[d]**. Repeat for the other end.

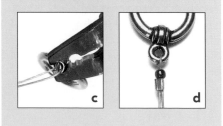

Wrapped loop connections

1 When I do wirework, I work from the coil so I don't waste wire by cutting ahead of time. String a bead onto the coil. With chainnose pliers, grasp the wire 1 in. (26mm) from the end and make a right-angle bend **[a]**. Position the jaws of the roundnose pliers at the bend and use your fingers to wrap the wire around the jaw and up **[b]**. Open the loop slightly and string a second component **[c]**. This is the first half of a wrapped loop.

2 Grasp the loop with the tip of the chainnose pliers and finish wrapping the loop with two or three wraps **[d]**. Trim and tuck the end **[e]**. Slide the bead you strung in step 1 until it rests next to the wraps. Continuing to work from the wire coil, make a right-angle bend ⅛ in. (3mm) above the bead **[f]** and make another wrapped loop above the bead **[g]**.

3 Repeat step 1 to string a third component and make the first half of a wrapped loop, linking it to the wrapped loop above the bead **[h]**. Repeat step 2 to finish the wraps.

4 Continue linking components in this way, including half a clasp **[i]**.

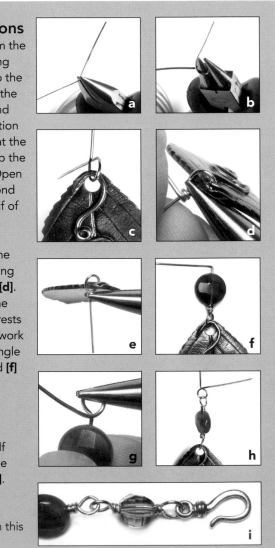

Drying setup

Metal clay needs to be completely dry before it can be fired, otherwise moisture in the clay will cause cracks or breaks. You can let pieces dry overnight or speed the drying time by using low heat.

If you are making just a few flat pieces at a time, a **mug warmer** is an inexpensive but effective choice. A **griddle** set to the lowest possible temperature (about 150°F/66°C) gives you more surface area. Turn the pieces over occasionally as they dry. Most pieces will dry within 20–25 minutes. Look for a uniform light coloration – dark areas indicate moisture is still present, which could crack the piece if fired prematurely.

For larger pieces, use a **food dehydrator**. Thorough drying may take 30 minutes or more, depending on the thickness of the clay and the complexity of the piece. A dehydrator is also good for drying leaves and seed pods before covering them with slip.

Kiln setup

I use a small, programmable electric **kiln**. Items in the kiln rest on a shelf. Always use **tongs** to place items in a preheated kiln and to remove items from a hot kiln. **Vermiculite** supports dimensional pieces, allowing them to retain their shape during firing. To hold the vermiculite, use inexpensive

FIRING METAL CLAY Fire longer at a higher temperature for the most shrinkage and durability.

Clay type	Minimum firing temperature	Minimum firing time	Shrinkage	Firing method
PMC3 (If the piece includes glass, fire from cold kiln)	1290°F (700°C) 1200°F (650°C) 1110°F (600°C)	10 min. 20 min. 45 min.	10–12%	Butane torch or kiln
PMC+ Sheet	1650°F (900°C) 1560°F (850°C) 1472°F (800°C)	10 min. 20 min. 30 min.	10–12%	Kiln
PMC Standard	1650°F (900°C)	2 hours	25–30%	Kiln

💡 *Do not use any equipment for food preparation after use with metal clay.*

clay saucers because they will crack after one or two firings.

A **butane torch**, the same kind used in making crème brûlée, can be used to fire small pieces (no larger than a dime) made from PMC3.

Polishing setup

When silver clay is fired, the surface appears white. Polishing smooths the reflective particles in the metal, revealing a shiny silver surface.

Brushing the fired piece with a **wire brush** and **soapy water** works to polish the metal, but if you want faster results, use either a **rotary tumbler** with stainless steel shot and burnishing compound, or a **magnetic polisher** with polishing media.

programmable kiln

butane torch

mug warmer

vermiculite

Tips and Techniques

Keeping metal clay moist

Metal clay in lump form dries out very quickly, so make every effort to keep it moist and malleable. Remove only what you need from the package, and immediately wrap the remaining portion in plastic wrap. Keep a mister handy while you're working with it and spritz the clay from time to time to keep it fresh.

To keep syringe clay fresh, always store an opened syringe tip-down in a cup of water. It's always a good idea to keep a cup of water, a brush, and a paper towel at your side while working with metal clay.

Rolling metal clay

Lightly grease a plastic mat and roller, and place the clay on the mat between two equal stacks of cards. You can put a plastic mat or plastic wrap over the clay to help it retain moisture as you roll. Keep the ends of the roller resting on the cards to ensure evenly rolled clay.

Working with casting grain

Many of my metal clay pieces are embellished with casting grain. Attach these little balls of precious metal with syringe clay. I generally use silver casting grain, but it also is available in other metals, including 24k gold, rose gold, and copper.

Handling and sanding

Once the clay has dried, it can be fragile. Work gently and carefully when filing, adding holes, and sanding.

Do the majority of your sanding before firing the piece; dry, unfired clay is much easier to sand than fired clay. Pay special attention to sanding the insides of rings to make them smooth. To avoid wasting clay, hold pieces over a container of slip of the same type of clay. The clay dust will settle into the slip.

Adding your signature

If you wish to sign your piece or add your initials, use a needle stylus to sign it before firing. Lightly scratch the surface and then go over it again once or twice, removing a small amount of clay.

Kiln-safe materials

Cubic zirconia (CZs) and synthetic corundums can be fired in the kiln at any of the recommended temperatures for any PMC product.

Glass cabochons, including dichroic glass, can be fired in the kiln with PMC3 products at PMC3-recommended temperatures. Most glass begins to flow at 1400°F (760°C), and therefore it is not recommended that you use PMC+ products with glass.

Porcelain can be fired in the kiln at any of the temperatures recommended for PMC products. Because the glazes used on porcelain may have different reactions at higher temperatures, it's safer to fire at lower temperatures or test-fire an extra glazed piece similar to the one you're planning to use.

Adding a patina

I love the beautiful colors that result from using a liver of sulfur solution on metal clay. Colors can range from blues, golds, and purples all the way to black.

Though liver of sulfur is nontoxic, its powerful odor of rotten eggs can be unpleasant. Use it in a well-ventilated room and avoid inhaling the fumes.

I prefer the dry form of liver of sulfur over the liquid – it stays fresher longer and a little goes a long way. To use, place a very small chunk in just enough hot water to cover the metal clay piece. When the chunk has dissolved, use tweezers to dip your piece in the solution. You'll see colors begin to appear, and when the piece is a color you like, remove it and rinse with cold running water. Use a polishing cloth or pad to remove some of the patina.

Each session produces slightly different results. I usually just see what colors result and choose beads that complement the colors. If you aren't happy with the results, refire the piece or use a tarnish remover to take off the patina and try again.

Working with syringe clay

Controlling syringe clay can be a challenge. The best way is to let ¼–½ in. (7–13mm) dangle from the end of the tip **[a]** and simply let it drop in place onto your piece **[b]**. You always can nudge it slightly with a wet brush **[c]**. To make a dot or blob, touch the syringe to the piece and squeeze out clay to the size you want **[d]**. If you're having difficulty stopping the syringe flow, use a needle stylus to break it.

Syringes come filled and ready to use. Keep your syringes tip-down in water whenever they are not in use.

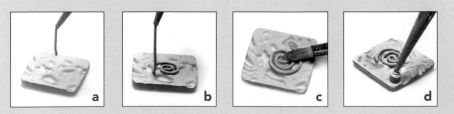